A GIRL'S WINTER IN INDIA

A GIRL'S WINTER IN INDIA

MARY THORN CARPENTER

GYAN

Published by

GYAN

Gyan Publishing House
5, Ansari Road
Daryaganj, New Delhi-110002
Phone: 011-47034999, 9811692060
E-mail: books@gyanbooks.com

Distribution Network
gyanbooks.com
India, USA, Canada, UK, Australia

ISBN: 978-93-7169-353-0 (PB)

First Published, 1892

2nd Impression 2025

Printed at: Gyan Press, Delhi.

GIRL'S WINTER IN INDIA
Author: MARY THORN CARPENTER

AN INDIAN RAJAH.

A GIRL'S WINTER IN INDIA

BY

MARY THORN CARPENTER

With Illustrations

NEW YORK
ANSON D. F. RANDOLPH & COMPANY
(INCORPORATED)
182 FIFTH AVENUE

To my Father,

FOR WHOSE PLEASURE THIS JOURNAL WAS WRITTEN; THAT
DESPITE THE DISTANCE SOMETHING IN IT MAY HELP
HIM TO SEE WHERE HIS EYES CANNOT REACH,
FOR WE HAVE "NEVER THE TIME AND
PLACE AND THE LOVED ONE
ALL TOGETHER."

MILLBROOK,
DUTCHESS COUNTY, N. Y.

"Only a learner,
A quick or a slow one;
Just a discerner,
I would teach no one."

CONTENTS.

CHAPTER I.

NAPLES AND THE MEDITERRANEAN.

CHAPTER II.

PORT SAID AND THROUGH THE SUEZ CANAL.

CHAPTER III.

ON THE INDIAN OCEAN.

CHAPTER IV.

THE ISLAND OF CEYLON.

CHAPTER V.

IN A SINGALESE PARADISE.

CHAPTER VI.

BOMBAY.

CHAPTER VII.

ALLAHABAD.

CHAPTER VIII.

CALCUTTA.

CHAPTER IX.

BENARES AND THE BRAHMINS.

CHAPTER X.

AT LUCKNOW AND CAWNPORE.

CHAPTER XIV.

A WELSH RAREBIT.

CHAPTER XV.

JEYPORE, THE CITY OF THE RAJPUTS.

CHAPTER XVI.

AN ELEPHANT RIDE TO AMBER.

LIST OF ILLUSTRATIONS.

A GIRL'S WINTER IN INDIA.

CHAPTER I.

NAPLES AND THE MEDITERRANEAN.

December 1, 18—.

PROSPER MERIMÉE, writing of the transition from Rome to Naples, said: "It is comedy succeeding tragedy," — which is certainly a vivid comparison. However, at night one city looks very much like another. Reaching Naples about seven in the evening, we were driven through the ruts and holes of the Neapolitan streets by a most circuitous route to the Hotel Grande Bretagne, opposite a beautiful park, that Watteau might have painted as a background for his stately ladies. Leaving the Roman Campagna, the railroad journey was through a succession of blue Albanian mountains, their rugged peaks softened by filmy clouds, while the greenest of grasses and climbing roses bordered the hillsides, until now we are in Naples, more dear and dirty than poet or realist ever described.

This morning the sun burst through our rooms; and rushing to the window, we saw, full in front, the matchless Bay of Naples, and the blue islands beyond, so soft in coloring, and bluer still than the deep blue water and the cloudless sky above them. The day proved sunny and warm, and we ordered a pair of good horses for a drive to Pompeii. The courier stows away our lunch in the big landau, leaps to a seat beside the driver, and with a scream to the horses we are flying down toward the bay. The air was delightful and breezy, although the wind sometimes came in gusts and stirred up the dust of the road. In the distance are the purple hills, bleak and rugged, where a white patch on a seemingly inaccessible point means a convent retreat of some Neapolitan sisterhood. Out on the wide streets which lead into the town there was life and bustle, and all the sights and sounds of human activity. Donkeys, with panniers of fresh green vegetables on each side, bigger than the best of them, were trotting to the market-place, their gayly studded harness surmounted on the saddle with brass weather-vanes, which answer purposes of color and usefulness. Little Neapolitan children, sitting at the doors of their houses bronzed and happy, were busy plaiting baskets; while the older girls, with kerchiefs and little peasant caps, sit demurely with their knitting. Farther on, among the suburban gardens, are the villas. And to show how perfectly impartial and honest a woman can be, I am willing to confess that the villas look much dilapidated. The pink stucco is falling off in unsightly patches, and the gardens are overrun with weeds, making a wilderness of orange and lemon-trees growing rank and wild among the palms. The names of the villas have a most transplanted look, — a wandering air, — as you read on the pillared gateways of a neglected, half-ruined mansion an inscription in English letters, "Villa, Sweet Home."

One cannot imagine a sadder sight than Pompeii. I will only mention the one thing which forces you to realize that this still and quiet place of the dead was once filled with intense life and movement of the splendid old Roman days. This is the pavement of the roadways, which is worn away in deep ruts, where the chariots once rolled in their great processions. The streets are lined with marble houses; the pavements, corridors, courts, and chambers are so well preserved that in a day or two workmen could put them in condition for occupation. Time has spread over the frescoed walls no dim varnish of age, and the color, which takes its name from the old city, is as bright to-day as when it was laid on by the Roman artist. Nothing that Nature has wrought, even in Italy, is quite so perfect as the country about Pompeii. There is such a profusion of waving palms, such clumps of orange and lemon trees, such mossy old buildings under a luxuriant trellis of grapes and leaves, although the dust has whitened each poor little leaf, and the summer sun has scorched and yellowed the vines. It would have seemed a perfect enchantment to live there; but the burning, smoking mountain, like a grim death's-head, is always present in the landscape, picturesque beyond the power of words to describe, but weird and oppressive, so that we shivered when the flame and smoke seemed to shoot up more briskly, driving down the fire and stones in our direction, and we wondered why the hill-dwellers on its stony sides did not seem to mind it, although they must be powdered snow-white at times by the dusty lava. Sometimes their dwellings seem entirely blotted out with the dense clouds of smoke; but when Vesuvius shows a bright flame against the evening sky, the people know it for a welcome sign. No earthquakes ever occur with the mountain in eruption.

We passed hours walking through the excavated streets, where they show you Diomede's lordly house and the Museum, where the petrified victims are stretched out in their dying agonies, in glass cases, gazed upon by the curious, as in a morgue. Here is the poor hound who met the same fate as his master, turned to stone, his legs drawn up in an attitude of most hideous suffering. And we hurry away from these painful sights to Augustus's Temple, where we rested and ate our luncheon gladly on the tiled floor in the room where the priest lived. It is quite impossible to see all the interesting things in Pompeii, but we do not regret it; there remains enough to form an impressive souvenir. Pompeii is the open sesame to the ancient world, as if by magic the past has been summoned to appear before us, and one is instructed and interested here beyond any place in all the world.

We have many things to attend to before taking the ship, letters to write, boxes to label; and so return in haste, for to-morrow we will be saying, "Addio, la bella Napoli."

December 6.

A great black ship lay at anchor off the curving shores of the Bay of Naples; and on the crowded wharf, among the coral venders, orange stalls, and idle sailors, were three Americans, guarding numerous boxes and packages to be put on board the Indian steamer by the little tug, flying the Peninsular and Oriental colors — a square, checkered with blue, white, yellow, and red — on her masts. On board the "Chusan," the dimensions are more those of an immense yacht, half the size of our enormous Atlantic steamers, but for that matter much more agreeable, having no throbbing motion of powerful machinery or the continual shiver of the screw. Her tonnage registers only 4,496, which we were surprised to find in a ship stanch enough to take us through the Mediterranean, down the Red Sea, and over the Indian Ocean. A number of natives, Lascars, Hindus, and Mahometans line the ship's deck. All the sailors are Orientals, as well as the stokers; and the rough work of the ship is done by Lascars, for English seamen would be utterly unfit for the climate we are coming to in a few days. The native sailors were in most summery attire, wearing picturesque red turbans, with white trousers reaching scarcely to their bare brown knees, and sometimes a scant over-garment girdled about with gayly colored sashes. In the large and well-lighted saloon below, the passengers were having four o'clock tea, and hugely enjoying themselves; but most of our fellow passengers had landed here to see Naples, and break the monotonous journey from London. The smoking-rooms are large and airy, the decks are clean, with wide promenades reaching almost from stem to stern; and when we finally explore our cabin, and find it well lighted by a big square port-hole, roomy and luxurious, with table, and even chairs, we begin to think our floating home for these next four weeks promises well, — and so it proves. Peninsular and Oriental officers are a very steady, well-trained set of men; but with all the strict discipline prevailing on board, the captain seems to run the ship for the pleasure of the passengers, forming with his officers a self-appointed committee to provide endless amusements. The Anglo-Indians on board also join with real English zest in games of quoits, where you endeavor to throw rings of rope into buckets placed a few yards apart on the deck. It requires skill and patience to succeed; and then, if you like, there is the game of "Bull." Who that has been on a Peninsular and Oriental steamer ever forgets the excitement of a "Bull" tournament, in which half-a-dozen or more players strive to cover, in turn, one of ten numbers on an inclined board; no easy task when the ship is rolling and tossing about. A double canvas stretches over our heads, and shades the sunny side of the deck. Under these awnings something is always going on,— pleasant chats in quiet corners, music on the piano in the companion-way saloon, people lying out in Eastern bamboo chairs reading, the staid English matrons quietly enjoying the serious business of a rubber at whist;—so the days pass. The weather cleared up directly we left Naples; and since then the sea has been very smooth, quite like the lazy Hudson in summer. The first morning out from Naples we passed quite close to Sicily, and steamed slowly through the Straits of Messina. Far over the quiet waters one could trace the little white dwellings clinging to the hillside, which we were informed was the busy town of Messina. It does not seem from this distance to be in the least astir, or doing anything else but dreaming in the sunshine.

> "All hushed—there is not a breeze in motion;
> The shore is silent as the ocean."

Later in the afternoon we could trace where Etna could be seen, had it not been covered in white fleecy veils, *à l'Arabe.* On a nearer view the faint blue line resting so lightly on the horizon would have materialized into the Island of Crete. But all the best field-glasses on board failed to discover for us the haven of Crete; and although the south wind blew softly, the modern mariners risked not the tempestuous breeze, called Euroclydon, which tossed the Alexandrian captain sailing into Italy. "Whose ship was caught, and could not bear up into the wind, so we let her drive." This is St. Paul's nautical report of his shipwreck. The ordinary weather along this shore is frightful; and it is always a chance if a sudden tempest may not come tearing down upon the ship, bringing us the same fate as Cæsar's prisoner. But to-day the sun and sea are wooing Britomartis (a Cretan nymph, who threw herself into the waves just at this very spot), and are on their very best behavior. The sly, deceitful, little ripples look very harmless in their calm blue depths, as if they never intend to become mountains of rolling billows. Truly, as Holmes says, "the sea remembers nothing; it is feline, — it licks your feet, its huge flanks purr very pleasantly for you, but it will crack your bones and eat you for all that; and wipe the crimson foam from its jaws as if nothing had happened."

What a delightful sensation it is to get one's bearing, to saunter up and down the wide deck, with nothing more imperative to do than to bask in the warm sunshine, or discover a congenial spirit among your fellow passengers, with whom you chat pleasantly for an hour, to pass away the time. The ship's company are being shaken together, and becoming more companionable at this stage of the voyage. On board are Anglo-Indians going to Calcutta, merchants, servants of Her Majesty, civil or military, with a sprinkling of tourists doing the trip around the world; but they (the Anglo-Indians) know what they are talking about, and have rare bits of information about India not to be found in any book. The "Chusan" is a very properly-conducted English ship; but, of course, we have every shade of clergyman on board, in color and sect; so, this morning, there were two rival church services going on at the same hour in different parts of the ship; and two more Dissenters are Presbyterianizing and Wesleyanizing their forces for the outdoing of the Church of England to-night. They have been fearfully disturbed by the "right of way," which the English Church claims on all Peninsular and Oriental boats; and, especially, they have now great cause for discontent in the persecution they suffer from the daily English morning service.

The more I see of the ship's people, the more I like them. At the head of our table sits a commissioned officer from Assam, the high borderland of the Himalayas; next, the Queen's attorney-general, of Hong Kong; then, a tea planter, who has lived years in Ceylon, been a resident in China, and whose present occupation is unknown. Our companions at table are frequently quite in the dark regarding the things which we Americans talk about. "What is a clam?" asked a Scotchman, who is going to Ceylon. "Is it a small kind of apple?" This, apropos of our description of fried and scalloped clams, brought out a peal of laughter from the English, who are not supposed to be easily moved to signs of surprise or amusement in public; but I find them gay and good-humored, and appreciative of a good story. A ship's officer told the following at dinner last evening: —

"As a rule, all engineers on steamers are Scotchmen; and once a man wagered he could go down in the engine room, and call out 'Mac,' and some one would answer. Then he went to the door of the engine room, and called loudly, 'Mac!' No one replied, until after a pause some one spoke up, 'Mon, which of the five Macs do you mean?'"

We are steaming very slowly, only twelve miles an hour; and after three impatient days we sail up to Port Said and the entrance to the great Canal.

CHAPTER II.

PORT SAID AND THROUGH THE SUEZ CANAL.

PORT SAID, December 10.

WE reached Port Said yesterday at twelve o'clock, in a pouring rain; but when our big anchor was let down, the sun came out, a light breeze tempered the mid-day heat, and Port Said, with its rich red soil and clumps of brilliant palms, was before us, making a splendid contrast to the sea. What we saw was a low, dirty town, with the sea running quite close to its principal street, where the sails of all colors and nationalities were crowded close to the habitations of the children of the soil. Little boats with their Arabian owners crowded around the ship, for the chance of taking us on shore. We have entered quite well up in the Canal. Near us are many ships; and a Turkish man-of-war runs up her crescent, while a companion ship, the "Shannon," is undergoing the process of coaling, which sounds prosaic enough, but is most interesting. Fancy a low black barge close up to the ship's sides, connected with it by black planks, over which men pass up and down like dark flashes, the coal-dust outrivalling their dusky skins, all dressed alike in ghoulish garments, with black scarfs floating from their heads. I never saw anything more impish than these swift creatures of darkness appearing and disappearing quickly from the depths of the "Shannon," carrying black baskets, grimy with the coal from years of service.

The next affair was landing. B. and I had long ago grown tired of the confinement of the ship; and we are to stay here six hours to coal. So we are rowed across the little bit of muddy water to Port Said, for an exorbitant sum, by Arab boatmen in gay and fantastic head-gear. With us was a young German officer and a Church of England rector, on his way to the Church college at Agra. Port Said is a picture of discomfort and misery. No one but the wild Arabs live here on the borders of the desert, where nothing grows that I can perceive except the ever-present palm-trees, that do their best to adorn the queer little straggling town that is striving for existence. Beneath our feet are many inches of red and muddy soil, but the streets are novel and picturesque. We are in Africa indeed, — an Africa of veiled women, each wearing a great brass tube over her forehead just between the eyes, the better to conceal her features, and clad in sombre drapery of black or dark blue over head, arms, and the entire figure, the better to follow out Mahomet's command that the women should be kept in seclusion. A quarter of the town was occupied by the market-women, who squatted along the roadside, among dirty rugs and heaps of green vegetables, and sold chicory, oranges, and fish.

Some one proposed a donkey ride, and it seemed a most attractive suggestion. So we communicated our intentions to the nearest donkey-boy, and soon had the whole town running after us with their donkeys, screaming in broken English the merits of their beasts. Donkeys seemed to blow from every quarter of the heavens at once. It was demoralizing. Each man was as keen and sordid about the suitable compensation for a donkey ride as in the most civilized community. The Arabian donkey-men are tall, with beautiful erect carriage, shapely bare arms and legs, with some sort of coarse white drapery worn about their bodies, covering them from shoulder to knee in folds which would delight a sculptor. The general appearance of the donkeys was forlorn, the saddles shabby beyond description, although they looked as if in their best days they had been very pretentious with gold embroidery and silver tassels. The donkeys know their owners' voices as well as possible, and answer to every cry and kick of encouragement from their drivers as they scamper along. Each donkey had its name: mine was Mrs. Langtry, B.'s Parnell, and another was

"What a pair of lovely black eyes." They evidently have caught this latter expression from having heard it so often applied to themselves. Imagine our donkeys galloping along, and the Arabs running beside them, out on the ocean of sand. It was a desolate country we passed through, — a scattered Arab dwelling here and there, or a mosque farther on; and the most populous place seemed to be the Arab burying-ground, where the poor wretched natives are brought in great numbers from their malarious, fever-stricken Port Said. No green trees or bushes grow in the distant sandy miles before us; only an immense solitude, a cobalt sky, and the yellow desert sand. The Arabs have a most acute sense of humor, and apply the name of "Mr. Masher" to our young rector, who is vastly amused. "Go on, Mrs. Langtry," shrieks the Arab, when her namesake attempts to lag or slacken the pace. "Don't let Mr. Parnell get ahead." "Hi, hi, walk along, Labouchere," is addressed to a stout little donkey between blows from the driver's stick. In vain did I feel my dignity was fast disappearing with every inch of the road; in vain was I warned by streaming hair and floating bits of apparel. It was all too perfectly enchanting to care for appearances, and I could have galloped on forever. Every one was sorry when it came time to return; but it consoled us a little to partake of Turkish coffee before leaving, and lay in a stock of fans for the Red Sea. The ship is hauling up anchor, and dinner is served, so I will put up the journal for to-day, and spend the evening looking out upon the Canal. Good night, Port Said.

December 12.

Port Said owes its name to an Egyptian Pasha, and its existence to the Suez Canal; its port forming the entrance to the Canal from the Mediterranean Sea. There is a decided bustle and air of activity in the place, from the noise of Arabs bringing coal to the ships, and the daily departure of tourists to the different ports of the Holy Land, Syria, and the East.

De Lesseps has said that during his stay in Egypt, as consul for the French government, he conceived the idea of bringing the two hundred millions of Europeans and the seven hundred millions of Asiatics in closer relationship, by the erection of a sea canal across the Isthmus of Suez. This was in the year 1856; and until its completion in 1869, the great French engineer encountered difficulties, financial and political, which would have deterred the most optimistic Englishman. "Notre entreprise n'a que deux ennemis, le sable et l'espace," said an enthusiastic Frenchman; but these were mute and tractable enemies, mere nothings to the hostile forces to be overcome, — the opposition of the Ottoman Porte and England's "sealed coffers." But the magnetic personality of De Lesseps persuaded and fascinated every one connected with the affair, from the French bankers to the Arabian sheiks. The advantage to England from the Canal, which was at first so bitterly discouraged by her statesmen, is now simply inestimable. The increase of British commerce with the East is about forty millions sterling. In avoiding the Cape of Good Hope and coming through by the Suez Canal, the steamships save a distance of four thousand, four hundred and forty-five miles, going from London to Bombay; and indeed the business of the whole world has been changed.

An English nobleman, invited by the Khedive to witness the opening of this great engineering achievement, describes what must have been as startling a scene as any ever played by her children in Egypt, the Mother of the World. "We then went to the religious ceremony of the benediction of the work. There was a large stand, in front of which sat the Khedive, the Empress of the French, the Emperor of Austria, and a dozen small royalties; and behind the Empress, stood — guess who? — Abdul Kader, in his burnouse, covered with decorations — a most striking figure. Opposite the stand were two others, one with a Moslem pulpit turned toward Mecca, and the other with a Catholic altar. The Moslem began the prayers, every one remaining covered; and when he had done, there was a Catholic service to bare heads."

We leave Port Said during dinner, and at once enter the Canal. A striking moment it was — to my mind, the grandest of the journey. During the evening we go on deck, and look out on the electric light, which is placed in our bow, and can be seen for miles. An extra pilot has also been taken on board, and a suitable rudder; all three will be left at Suez. A sand storm approaches later, and a high wind has arisen. The captain has ordered the ship tied up. Natives go ashore and fasten the "Chusan" to one of the big ship posts that line the Canal for this purpose; and sand, thick like a fog, is about us, filling our eyes and every nook of the steamer with the little glinting particles. We pass the evening with games, singing, and private theatricals, in which every one contributes, and wind up with a Swedish dance something like our Virginia Reel. From my cabin window, in the bright moonlight, I can distinguish files of rats crossing and re-crossing the huge ropes which fasten our ship to the shore, drawn clearly against the shaft of electric light shining from the bows, as the ancient rats embroidered Proserpine's veil.

Up with the anchor, and before seven o'clock next morning we are off once more. From the deck we see Lake Menzalah on both sides, then through the narrow part, often not more than seventy-five feet wide. The whole day we traverse the solemn, quiet desert. I think every one who has made the journey will agree with me that the great ship moving through the silent desert is the grandest experience one has ever had. The "Chusan" makes six miles an hour through the Canal; and on the sandy banks we can see the moving figures of pitiful half-clad Arabs, who keep up well with the ship, and clap their bony hands, crying "backsheesh," keeping step in time with a strange, unearthly hum. The English pennies thrown from the deck are followed with eagle eyes, and seized before they reach the sand. How these barbarians exist on the edge of the desert, — not a sign of a human dwelling or a green thing for miles, nothing but uninterrupted waste of sand, — no one could tell us.

The sand storm has been disastrous along the route. A Russian man-of-war, and still another Peninsular and Oriental boat, are tied up or aground in the sand, blown out of the narrow channel. As we go on, a boat from Ismailia comes to take off passengers for Cairo, who fling back many a good-by to those left standing by the ship's railing, watching the tug steam away and finally disappear. The town is supplied with fresh water by a canal from Cairo, and looks very pretty from this distance, with its green clumps of palm-trees and shrubbery — a wilderness made to blossom for the pleasure of the Khedive. The little

Bitter Lakes — so called from a certain alkali contained in the waters — are now widening before us. It was here that the waters of the Red Sea and the Mediterranean met; and some one has remarked that "their respective fishes must have been rather astonished to make acquaintance." The waters of the Mediterranean are salter than the Atlantic, and the Red Sea salter still, due I believe to the great evaporation which takes place under a tropical sun, no fresh water supplying its place. In olden times the Red Sea extended to the Bitter Lakes; and it was there the Israelites crossed it. The northern portion of this sea is now called the Gulf of Suez.

We are approaching Mecca; not far away lies Judea, and on the other hand is the land of the worship of Isis and Osiris. The Red Sea is a great contradiction in color. No one has explained its name, unless "Red" means "fiery;" although many historians agree that it takes its name from the shores which border the desert, and are reddish in color. The scenery here is most peculiar — bare hills, without a single tree or trace of vegetation to be seen in any direction. Mt. Sinai is before us: we see its summit very clearly, although the captain says it is two miles from the shore. It is not the highest peak of the mountain range by any means, but one of a group of three, and lower than its companion, Mount St. Catherine. A cloud is resting there very softly, and almost hides its face, as in ancient times there appeared over the Mount a thick cloud because of the Presence there. We cannot see the plain where the children of Israel were encamped, but the formation of the country is exactly that described in Scripture, especially where the children of Israel crossed the Red Sea. You can see there was only one thing to do — mountains in the south hemmed them in, on the north the Egyptian army was sweeping down in great numbers, forcing them to pass through the sea as a "last resort." On the borders of the desert were some great camels, lying down with their huge burdens, resting from the long journey. They looked the perfect "ships of the desert," as they are so often called.

They tell us this is quite exceptional weather for this portion of the journey; our cabin thermometers register only 70°, and on deck it is even less, only 65° in the shade. This sea is supposed by travellers to be "the hottest place in the world; the wind is generally like a sirocco, and the water becomes so heated that it often seriously interferes with the condensation of steam." During the hot season, the heat becomes so intense that here on the "Chusan" six persons have often died in one morning from sunstroke or apoplexy. The captain said expressively this morning that men sometimes died on the tables which were afterwards set for breakfast. Often all the stokers and engineers are down, and there remains no one to keep up the fires. Certainly the bakers and stokers have the hardest time. Already the officers are beginning to appear in white duck trousers and very *négligé* attire; while the Anglo-Indians, who have realized the ideal of comfort, are wearing large Terai hats, white silk shirts, and show a decided dislike for any violent exercise.

On Sunday morning the service was conducted on deck by the Rev. Mr. H. and another. The officers and stewards and the second cabin passengers came up to attend it. There are sixteen missionaries in the second cabin besides the clergy on board, one of whom goes out to India as principal of a native high-caste college at Agra, with four hundred students. All over the ship a lively conversation is kept up on the subject of missions — a subject quite strange to the usual talk on steamers, but aroused by the presence on board of so many zealots, who seem to call out special antagonism from the Anglo-Indians every time their stiff white collars and broad-brimmed hats appear in view. The general opinion of residents near the mission fields seems to be that the native is not easily converted to Christian ideas, but that the missionaries undoubtedly form a great civilizing power in the East. The Hindu religion admits that Christianity is all very good ; and they adopt it along with their own, arguing that the principle of religion remains the same, and the outward forms do not matter. A Hindu believes all proceeds from the Almighty, and all is in him. They may worship their ancestors, or set up a limb of a tree and perform their devotions before it. Only yesterday I heard a story of a man in Southern India who was seen to bow down to the tomb of an English general and make an offering of brandy and soda, considered by the observing native the most appropriate tribute to the Englishman's well-known taste.

CHAPTER III.

ON THE INDIAN OCEAN.

ADEN, December 17.

EARLY Tuesday morning we passed Perim, the rocky island which "guards the gates of the Red Sea," and during the day had many glimpses of the bare profiles of uninhabited islands, sharp and half sunken, appearing to float on the water like stony icicles, making navigation both dangerous and difficult; and in the old days there were more wrecks in coming here than in any other part of the world. Threading our way through the pointed rocks of this little archipelago, we sighted the island of Mocha on our left,—an uninhabited desert: no living soul was to be seen, no trace of life or vegetation; even the Arabian growers of the famous coffee had abandoned their torrid little island to its primitive desolation. It was the captain's trained seaman's eye which first discovered Aden, far away on the horizon, and the English rector, the queen's attorney, B. and I, and others, who were going to India for the first time, crowded about him in an excited group, straining our eyes and levelling our glasses at that barren point of rock and sand lifted in such fantastic outlines above the Arabian Sea. In a few moments the bleak and rugged peaks shone forth one after the other more distinctly, bathed in a mellow light, which softened the outlines and did its best for Aden to make a good impression. The masts of many vessels are reflected in the clear blue waters of the harbor. A Russian corvette, painted white and gold, having on board the Czarowitch, is anchored near us, attended by a formidable fleet of boats, carrying guns of terrible calibre. An Englishman expresses the hope that this scheme of educational travel will serve to broaden the mind and liberalize the ideas of the future father of his people.

The sea is now swarming with a floating population of queer blacks and Mussulmans in boats, who soon take possession of the contents of our purses. The Arabs are selling curiously braided baskets, with secret compartments; and the Jews offer us ostrich boas of natural feathers, at an exorbitant price. What a combination of shrewdness, craft, and mercantile cunning is an Arabian Jew! A crowd of little Somalese boys, with nothing on to prevent their free movements, came off from the land in canoes and row-boats. They single out the tourists on the deck at a glance, and half-a-dozen or more call to us in persuasive accents, "Give us a dive,—yes, yes, yes,—give me a dive," their teeth gleaming clear as stars in a black night. For a two-anna bit the little fellows would dive from their dug out canoes, follow the flight of the coin through the water, and appear with it between their white teeth, shaking their wet, shaggy locks like water-dogs, and looking over the waves for their canoe. Now the greatest feat was to get into the canoe once more without upsetting it completely. Swimming with one hand on the boat, the little fellow would watch for a friendly wave, throw one foot quickly over, and at once begin to bale out the water with his hands and kick it out with both feet. The little black boys are the most wonderful swimmers and divers in the world, almost as much creatures of the sea as of the land. We are rowed ashore in big boats by natives, some with only about two yards of cloth and an amber necklace for clothes.

On the land the sun beats down, and the air seems to vibrate visibly with heat. Not a tree or shrub or a bit of grass has the courage to peer through the hot sand, to die in this withering atmosphere. I bought a rather good photograph of the many different nationalities which live in Aden, who are mostly recruited from the opposite shore of Africa. Nubians and Arabians form the only people fitted by nature to exist and thrive on these volcanic rocks. In vain are we warned of the certain and disastrous effect of the sun on venturesome sightseers in Aden. One must pass days at sea to understand the longing to set foot on terra firma once more. Even barren Aden seems in a way a paradise, and we can't waste a minute of precious time; so hail an inexpressibly queer vehicle, well covered over the top and sides with white muslin to divert the sun's rays, and motion the grinning native to follow up the one street of the town, — a semicircle of opium bazaars and shabby shops, with natives smoking long pipes at the doorways, while inside is displayed a forlorn collection of Arabian ostrich eggs, uncurled plumes, and badly-cured Ibex horns, — the specialties of the town, — all alike dingy and dirty with the fumes of the coarse tobacco.

We come suddenly on the camel market, where camels are drawing loads, harnessed to carts, and carrying immense burdens on their backs; and B. and I, who are always ready to enjoy any new and exciting amusement, are seized with an intense desire to ride a camel. Mr. L. consented to bargain with a tall Arabian in many-colored raiment, the owner of a camel which had never before been called on to grunt under a greater fardel than two packs of grain. Once secured, the beast was made to recline, and Mr. L. mounted first. I must confess that the sight of the venerable man, his white hair floating in the wind, clinging tightly to the camel as the beast commenced the operation of getting up, was a most ridiculous spectacle. The camel seemed to have several knees before the ordinary ones were reached, and kept going up, until we thought he would keep on indefinitely. From the shout that went up from the good-natured crowd gathered around us, I knew that this must be a most unusual and laughable spectacle, and I felt many misgivings of conscience that I should have been the cause of putting my good-natured companion to open shame. We start off, and the camel makes a simpering attempt at trotting, which we manage very well, and the entire population follow after us and urge the beast along. It is a motley crowd, with bare legs, but draped in bright shawls thrown over the shoulders, and nothing else, — a compromise between a dress and no dress at all. Some wore curious silver receptacles like snuff-boxes, fastened on the arm by silver chains, which serve them for purses, as their clothes — or rather the absence of clothes — admits of no pockets for small change. Running along in this most absurd procession are many little native black boys, — the *jeunesse ebène* of Aden, — with their little curly heads on one side.

They look up so beseechingly at us, making a kind of *meou*, at the same time rubbing their little bare chests to make us believe they are hungry, smiling all the while, knowing that it is for their picturesqueness only that you will be tempted to part with your silver. Some of our own ship's people had now joined the throng, and were gesticulating and laughing loudly; and a little later all witness the dismounting process. First, the beast gets down in front, but manages to keep up on his hind quarters; and this particular one objected in horrible sounds to getting down any lower, and we were thrown forward almost on our faces, when a few pricks and sticks from his owner persuaded the camel to reason. It was the oddest bit of travelling yet, and I wish I could make you all see the scene as I saw it. I could not help thinking how serviceable the faces of these barren and very prominent rocks would be to Pears' Soap or Sapolio. The English would make a pretty penny by it; some one should make the suggestion to Lord Salisbury.

We left Aden at sunset to-night. No words can describe the beauty of the scene from the bridge of the "Chusan," looking toward the setting sun. From all the boats the tired Mussulmans were washing in buckets of water, or having finished this important religious ceremony, were sometimes prostrate in the direction of Mecca, sometimes silhouetted in bronze against a pale orange sky. It was indescribably picturesque; and the scene was heightened by a small island of volcanic rocks in the foreground, ragged, ice-like peaks, outlined in black, and beyond, the lemon-colored horizon, and the dark indigo waters encircling the island. Soon the sunset deepens in orange and reds, the moon hangs a pendent silver crescent in the sky, and the stars come out.

INDIAN OCEAN.

Since we left Aden we have had a marvellously calm sea, that mirrors our masts in its glassy-like surface. No one can realize what it is to go on a voyage in these latitudes, unless you are here on the spot. Every day on the Arabian Sea has passed like a dream — a dream of the Castle of Indolence: even the captain seems to run the ship as if by magic; no discipline that we can see, no bustling orders, or fog-blasts, or tempests to trouble. Indeed, we never think of our ship-life as strange or unnatural: it is like our earth-life; and perhaps we shall not remember how to live on land again. The air seems to be growing hotter and hotter; we appear to be sailing straight away into tropic heat as we near the equatorial line. Little children play about the deck in old-fashioned, low-necked, and short-sleeved gowns; and the bare-footed *ayah* faithfully paces up and down, crooning softly Hindu lullabies to the little white baby, who has not even a fleecy shawl about its bare arms. We appear most comfortably in shirt waists, even to the second and third generations of grandmothers — everybody has adopted a silk blouse. During the day and night the port-holes are always open; and the steward places a square canvas wind-sail at your cabin port to catch any stray breezes at night.

I have retired under the punkah, which is being pulled in breezy sweeps by the handsome young Indian, who has inherited a tireless energy in pulling at a rope for hours. Since we left Port Said the punkahs have been going constantly in the saloon, where we betake ourselves often, only too thankful for an artificial breeze to aid us in writing up our correspondence and finishing our home-letters for the English mail-steamer at Ceylon. The tiffin has just ended; and from a long list of such unknown delicacies as "bubble and squeak," "prawn curry," and "jugged hare," we have declined everything provided by the Peninsular and Oriental company, except sardines and bread and butter, ending with oranges and a bottle of champagne, ordered to quell a rebellion of the internal elements, which is making our lives plainly miserable, since to-day we are rolling a trifle in the blue waves of the Indian

Ocean. The only news I can give you is that of waves, sky, and the white foaming track the ship is ploughing up through the latitudes and longitudes, the zones and meridians, of the greatest part of this earth's surface, which we call sea. We make, with a good wind to help on, about three hundred and twenty miles from twelve o'clock noon of one day to the same eight bells the next day. The nights are calm beyond words; the moonlight bright as day; and in the sky appear many unknown stars with strange and unfamiliar effects — even the Great Bear is turned upside down, making the heavens look strange and unnatural. The Indian Ocean is lit by a phosphorescent light, an intense emerald green; and the waters are clear, reflecting all the stars. I never knew anything more weird and dreamy than to stand in the bows and look out in the misty star-tangled air, followed by the serpent-like trail of the phosphorescent light. On her last trip, the ship just here speared a shark, twenty-six feet long, with her bow; and so firmly was the fish fastened in front, that the ship was stopped to dislodge it. Every night during dinner the quartermaster and the Lascar sailors clear the deck of everything movable, and cover every nook and corner with gay bunting and bright flags; so we find the ship changed as if by magic into an improvised ball-room. The last evening, the captain invites us formally to a ball. On shipboard, Saturday, as a rule, is baggage day, when the passengers are allowed to replenish their wardrobe from the boxes in the hold; but for this occasion the officers are ordered to haul up the luggage, to be ransacked for party finery. During the evening the dancing goes on merrily, and we enjoy numerous lemon squashs, proved to consist of lime-juice and soda-water — the Eastern substitute for lemonade. Songs, toasts, and an elaborate supper follow, for the prospect of ending our long voyage to-morrow has inspired every one with an unusual vivacity; and not until the morning hours did any of the dancers seek their repose in the cabins, or on the deck mattresses, provided for the occupants of the heated cabins, where sleep is impossible in the stifling atmosphere. B. and I went down among the last, with slow and reluctant steps, feeling that this was the last parting from friends, who three weeks ago were strangers, but of whom we shall always keep a bright memory.

CHAPTER IV.

THE ISLAND OF CEYLON.

COLOMBO, December 24.

IT was a warm, delicious night. For the last few hours every one had been in a frenzy of excitement, and our impatience to see land became uncontrollable. Suddenly a bright light flashed and reflected itself in the sea, and breezes from cocoanut and palm-trees floated fresh from the shore. "Colombo," shouted a sailor on the forward watch; "Colombo," echoed the captain from the bridge; "Colombo," repeated the passengers each to the other, with various shades of emotion; and at that word my own fancy created a whole city full of mystery and wonders. We ascended the hurricane deck, crowded the ship's bows, and leaned far over the railing, peering into the quiet night and breathing the cinnamon-scented air of Colombo, the capital of Ceylon. Scarcely a word was spoken; every face expressed a different emotion, but each was visibly changed. The voyage was ended. Something seemed reversed in our life's machinery. We had expected it to end, but had banished the idea to a dim future, as we do the Day of Wrath; and like that day, it came upon us as "a thief in the night," robbing the bread-winners of India of the needed rest before the battle for existence so soon to begin, and bringing the fledglings of future engineers abreast of their problems, and the boyish candidates for the forestry department face to face with jungles and giant trees in Burmah. Everything was indeed ended for the red-haired Peninsular and Oriental officer, whose hopes were being calmly annihilated in a quiet corner of the ship by a coquettish English girl, whose constant companionship on this voyage had induced a wish for the longer one through life. In the least frequented parts of the ship, other sad partings were taking place, for we were all more or less sentimentally affected by the dreamy moonlit evenings. Even the jolly young rector has declared himself "half a friend and all a lover" to his pretty partner in the cricket games; and at this stage of the voyage, the men who have promised to be B.'s "brothers" on the "Chusan," form quite a large family.

In the calm waters of the harbor, six large Peninsular and Oriental steamers lay moored; their masts and spars drawn clear against the bright sky; and the jetty lights from hundreds of cabin-ports outlined them from bow to stern, pouring forth bright gold on the dancing waters. All ships bound to Australia, or coming from China, remain at Colombo, to coal for the voyage; and the passengers from the different boats go ashore to join in an international dance at the Grand Oriental Hotel. When the clanking chains had let down the big anchor, impatience made us powerless to resist the temptation to land. To understand this, you must have travelled in Europe; found steamships puffing on the Grand Canal; have gazed on hideous modern structures, replacing the beautiful old castles on the Rhine; have paid your fare in a street car to visit the Roman Forum; and sought vainly in every nook and corner of the Continent for a spot uninvaded by modern notions.

And here before us was the changeless East,—the entrance into Wonderland,—and was it not "time elaborately thrown away" to remain on the ship and bemoan our past disillusions, instead "of having glimpses which might make us less forlorn?" Old travellers shake their heads at the idea of landing at night, and trusting our precious selves to the treacherous natives at this hour; and crabbed age and youth discuss the subject, until youth conquers, and we call a catamaran. A long, slim boat appears, rowed by six natives, wearing a waist-drapery of striped muslin, contrasting well with their bronzed skin. The boat fits you tightly on either side of the board seat, only wide enough for one person. And the quaint touch is the outrigging, which keeps the boat from capsizing by a balance-log of wood, intersected with ropes and bent poles, which touch the water, and are attached to the catamaran on one side only. Away we go; the Singalese making rapid headway over the ripples, bending their long necks forward and backward with the stroke, and showing their white teeth like flashes.

We were about midway across, when the boat suddenly stopped. One instant of sickening fright; the next, a wonder what was coming now. I see one of the heathen rise, and hear him shout something in strange sounding tones to the terrified attorney-general, accompanied by violent gestures. Is it robbery on the queen's highway? and I begin to wonder if my small silver would satisfy the brigands. Then a couple of natives forcibly make the trembling gentleman understand that he is to crawl out on the slender outrigging, the better to balance the boat. Nothing more dreadful occurs, and we all laugh at our sudden panic. At last we land at a sort of wharf projecting into the harbor, pass over that bit of red sand facing the Grand Oriental Hotel, are informed there is no room for us in the inn; and no choice left but to return to the "Chusan." The lights were out when we reached the ship; and we sought our cabins, stumbling over bundles of deck-sleepers, who proved by groans their unmistakable disapproval of such nocturnal disturbances — only to find our berths dismantled of everything, down to the mattress, and the cabin steward too fast asleep on the dining-room table to be aroused; so we repented our haste during that entire night. We went ashore early next morning, and were amazed to find the streets of Colombo crowded, the life of the shops in full swing, the banks and public buildings open, and the busy day well begun at half-past seven A. M.

Colombo is a babel of strange sounds and colors, all new and bewildering to me. Fancy a town of one hundred thousand blacks, — Singalese, Tamils, Mahometans and Hindus, — with only fifteen hundred Europeans. The natives wear a costume, if not the strangest, at least the most grotesque that one can imagine. The Singalese portion of the population are dressed in a dark coat, over a skirt of white muslin, fastened about the waist; their long black hair is brushed smoothly back from the forehead, and secured by a tortoise-shell comb, — the only feature which distinguishes the costume worn by the men from that of their wives, so far as I can see. Tea and bananas, our first chota-hazri, were served on the piazza of the Grand Oriental Hotel by a native servant, dressed in about a shilling's worth of white cotton cloth. Then we secured our rooms, and spent the morning in the bazaars.

An arcade extends along this low colonnaded caravansary, where the life of the town is concentrated. Here are the shops, the only apothecary, the only bookstand. Here, on the broad street, are congregated a long line of *jinrikishas*, the hansoms of Colombo. Groups of half-naked coolies squat on the ground, inert and motionless, scarcely distinguishable from a heap of dirty rags. Not allowed to approach nearer the hotel, they await the porter's signal; when, filled with sudden life, they jump quickly to a place between the shafts, and rush forward with the rickshaw. Here also are the jewellers' shops, where we were shown glittering heaps of precious stones, but found scarcely a good ruby or sapphire among them. Streeter, of London, and the great New York firms purchase all the valuable gems, leaving flawed and imperfect stones for tourists. No sooner has the unwary traveller set foot in the arcade, than these Moormen rush out of their shops, push a printed card of the firm in your hand, and press you to enter — no one escapes. Once inside, courtesy provides fans and chairs. You are soon seated at a table before heaps of sparkling rubies, cat's-eyes, pale sapphires, and moonstones. Then, if you like, bargaining begins, and a war of words is waged on the price. The insinuating jewellers produce well-thumbed letters from distinguished customers, Mr. Vanderbilt, or the Rothschilds, while they raise or lower prices in the scale of your enthusiasm. The least interest manifested in a particular stone on your part seals you as their prey. They hunt you for days, steal stealthily towards you at four o'clock tea on the veranda, and thrust the stone, shining on a bit of cotton-wool, directly under your eyes; or suddenly come upon you, just leaving for a drive, retreating from the blow of the porter's stick, only to re-appear more bland than before, — always polite, resenting nothing; they finally astonish you by accepting a tithe of the original price, and you are most fortunate if your gem proves not a bit of bright-colored glass. The barefooted rascals are cunning, and I am no match for them as far as I have gone. There are several good shops for tortoise-shell; here is the cheapest market in the world for shell, which the natives polish but never carve.

In the hotel, you feel transported to another planet. The building itself is not remarkable, resembling a large Italian house, white, low, and surrounded by balconies, with a beautiful garden, rich in flowering shrubs and brilliant trees; but the life and customs of the house are very Oriental, and suited to the tropics. We have an excellent table, — in the morning, *chota-hazri* (tea and toast, bananas and jam) is served in our room at six A. M.; breakfast (*burra-hazri*, or the big breakfast) comes at nine; tiffin at two; and dinner at the *table d'hôte* at eight. The great native *plât* is "curry": well, "curry" means anything, meat or vegetable, accompanied by miscellaneous dishes at the same time. Our "curry" of meat at dinner last evening was eaten with dried cocoanut, chutney simple and chutney green, Bombay duck (a funny little dried fish to be eaten with your fingers) rice, pulled bread, and turnover of potatoes, fresh yellow cocoanut, grated fine, white cocoanut sliced, besides the spices. All our servants are men; and are called, old and young indiscriminately, by one general name, "boy." It seems so absurd to call one of these grave, white-bearded Singalese, a "boy."

In the East, you are not expected to do anything for yourself, never to stoop or to cross the room: one call in the corridor brings a black multitude to your door, who know nothing but to serve you quickly and faithfully as a matter of course. I would give much for a picture of the Singalese barber who did the shampooing of my hair this morning, — straight as an arrow, in clinging white undergarment reaching to his bare feet, and a loose white coat; his front hair combed straight back under a narrow tortoise-shell comb. They all speak a few words of several languages, and understand better if one speaks broken English to them. I informed my native barber that I lived in America, not in England; and in wonder, he replied, "Lady speaks English very, very well."

COLOMBO, Christmas Day.

I was awake this morning at six o'clock, having it on my mind that Christmas had come in Ceylon. A very few fire-crackers and the church bells from the fort sounded outside my window; but by far the most noise was made by the birds in the garden trees who carolled away without ceasing. B. came in with Christmas greetings, and brought me a dainty chota-hazri, and soon we were both off in a gharri to the English church for eight o'clock service. The church, mossy and gray, is placed above the roadside in a dense palm grove. Among the congregation already in the church were high-caste native ladies, who occupied the benches, dressed in full low-necked and short-sleeved gowns; their bronzy black necks and arms quite covered with bracelets and jewelry. A drapery of white worked veiling covered the head, reaching to the waist; and a few wore old-fashioned and very scanty satin skirts. We passed many native grandees going to church in coaches, driven by black coachmen, in their white trousers, bare knees, and barefooted. Some Europeans drove very smart dog-carts, with black grooms standing behind, in bright red or yellow turbans and sashes; and all in white, without shoes and stockings. Indeed, everything in this climate is white. Carriages, and also umbrellas, are covered with white linen, as a protection against the sun's rays; even the residents appear in the evening for dinner in white linen clothes of English cut and make, and belted with red sashes, which look very bright in a drawing-room. In church, the service was read by the European chaplain from the fort; and the choir, organist and choristers, are all recruited from our dark brothers, the Singalese converts. For a reminder of Christmas, the church is festooned in white and green, while a couple of boys outside the open windows are pulling an immense punkah to and fro over the heads of the congregation; and from the doorway steals in the scented air of cinnamon gardens, and birds fly in and out of the windows, joining in carols and chants. "High noon behind the tamarisks; the sun is hot above us, as at home the Christmas Day is breaking wan."

December 26.

Another holiday, but rather a trying one for us, for the banks will not be open in three days for mail. To-day we drove out to an English bungalow in the cinnamon gardens, for four o'clock tea. These spicy gardens extend in every direction for miles, where white colonnaded bungalows are dotted here and there, half hidden in groves of feathery palms; where the Coleas make the hedges, and the roses of Sharon the shade trees. A bungalow in Ceylon means a low, thatched, one-story house, surrounded with piazzas nearly as large as the building itself, screened with mattings, and carpeted with bamboo rugs about the floor. The Ceylon tea is light in color, very mild and refreshing in this climate. After tea, we drove in Mrs. A.'s laudau to the museum. This, an exceedingly interesting one, is rich in native animals, tigers, elephants, and snakes, and also in curious jewelry, used for bridals and feasts by the ancient Kandians, who excelled in wondrously carved gold and silver work. A curious reminder of our own country were the masks, used even to-day by native Hindu priests for devil dances. They resemble those the medicine men depend on to drive away sickness among the Alaska Indians; the masks expressing different degrees of hideousness to charm away lameness, a man rushing away to kill himself, a fever-tormented person. This rude belief in charms and sorcery mingles the superstitions of far-away savages with pagan rites. Who can give a clew to this strange similarity?

An endless tide of every degree of Asiatic humanity ebbs and flows through the palm-fringed streets and sandy roads of Colombo. I am watching these crowds from my balcony, when a familiar sound comes to my ears: "Is the world going wrong?" A gay procession is coming down the dusty high-road, — a procession reviving childish Bible memories of Miriam, composed of one hundred barefooted maidens, in flowing yellow under-garments, turkey-red jackets, and the same pale yellow muslin floating from their pretty heads. They all have their tambourines, and shout as they pass: "We will do what we can," in the lively tune belonging to the hymn. The flaming banners of the Salvation Army are flying over the heads of the pale-faced English lasses, who, hoping to come more in touch with the natives, have adopted the Singalese dress and food, and live this self-sacrificing life. Unmindful of the noon-day sun, they march through the burning streets towards the pier, to greet other Salvationists, who land to-day in a special ship from England; and with more noise and the beating of drums, have recruited many picturesque additions of curious natives and children, in all colors and costumes, who join in the march to the barracks. The Army is said to be doing great good among the native people; and when we visited head-quarters, a sweet, soft-voiced English woman told us of her life here as a staff-officer. "It is marvellous," she said, "the kindness shown to us by the natives once you get near their hearts; and I dread going back to Europeans." She related to us a sad story of a young Tamil girl, whose mother desperately opposed her joining the Army, threatening to place her own head under a cart-wheel, unless the daughter returned to the faith. On her refusing, the mother ended her life in this way, but in vain, as the girl still remains true. Also a Parsee from Bombay has arrived here, who was almost killed by his people because of their hatred of this new religion. All these incidents show something of the opposition which General Booth's army encounters in the East.

What a collection of nationalities and tongues Ceylon possesses. First, the Singalese, known by tortoise-shell combs, long black hair, bare-headed under an umbrella of cotton; Tamils from Southern India, wearing more jewelry and white or red turbans; Mahometans, shaven and shorn under their funnel-shaped and many-colored bonnets; European planters with pale faces, or intensely burned and browned by the tropical sun; Buddhist monks, in yellow robes and shaven heads, munching a leaf of betel-nut and plying a palm-leaf fan, while behind them walks a little novice, all in white, who is carrying a cotton umbrella under his arm. England has here a rare collection of subjects, differing not only in their religion and country, their language and dress, but in opinions, ideas, and thoughts.

Without going back to Sinbad the Sailor, whose

adventures among the elephants of the Island of Ceylon are our delight; not even recalling the more prosaic Greeks, or Arabians, — we know that adventurous Portuguese visited Ceylon in the sixteenth century, and the colonizing Dutchmen, a hundred years later, left a permanent impression on the nomenclature of the beautiful island of Lanka. Among the shops are still many whose signs bear the hard Northern inscription. One might easily fancy oneself walking through the streets of The Hague, seeing the rows of sign-boards over the shops with distinctly Dutch names, similar to the one I have copied.

M. C. JOONOOS & CO.,

JEWELLERS,

AND

DEALERS IN PRECIOUS STONES,

No. 12 York Street,

COLOMBO, CEYLON.

Colombo has replaced the older town of Point de Galle as the capital of Ceylon. The streets are extremely wide, bordered with palm-trees, and with houses generally one-story high, having arcades, colonnades, and verandas; and many trees, and lawns planted with shrubbery, link together these quaint dwellings. Another afternoon we drove to the suburban annex of Colombo; here the rich tropical vegetation is cleared away in patches, and villas with backgrounds of cocoanut-trees and bananas spring up in every direction between the road and the ocean. The road winds through luxuriant foliage, with here and there lovely sea-views of the harbor, and the purple lights of the Indian Ocean stretching way beyond. Every bungalow has a boundless ocean view from its front door; and towards evening the merchants and men of business may be seen driving to these lovely homes in rickshaws drawn at a lively trot by native coolies, who are taking their masters home to sleep away the cares and fatigues of office life in the sweet-scented air and refreshing breezes of this beautiful spot.

These rickshaw coolies smear themselves once a week with cocoanut oil, so that it makes them impervious to the weather, draughts, or cold nights or rainy days. There is a general impression that the coolie will soon become as extinct a specimen as the mastodon, owing to lung troubles brought on by exposure in their scanty clothing to night winds. A movement was started this Christmas by the English Bishop for the purpose of providing cast-off coats for the use of the coolies, who are thoughtlessly left to stand in cold draughts, by their masters, after a sharp run, of perhaps miles, in the heat of the noon-day.

We returned past the Galle Face Hotel, half hidden behind the green foliage and fronting the ocean. Here we paused a few moments to breathe the delicious air and enjoy the magnificent view. It was a beautiful scene, — a tropical sunset. The sky faded, without one speck or cloud, from glorious orange, softening into pale violet. A silver moon was reflected in a lake on one side; the ocean, brilliant, intense, emerald, on the other. Separating the ocean from the lake was a mile of red, sandy driveway, only a hundred feet wide between the fresh lake and the dreary waste of ocean, and over all, the quiet and hush of Nature's lullaby, — "It were as if sunlight should shine out of deepest dark, illumining night's peace with daytime's glow."

December 29.

We have driven to Kalanie. It was necessary to make a very early start indeed; for in this hot climate the noon-day sun puts an end alike to business and pleasure after ten o'clock. A fresh air blew softly through the trees, stirring up an occasional puff of dust in the streets. Before starting out we picked up our Hindu guide from a motley crowd of natives at the entrance of the hotel, choosing one especially recommended for his linguistic talents. It was soon evident that our information concerning the various points of interest *en route* would be conveyed to us in a choice vocabulary of ten very broken, very imperfect, almost unintelligible English words possessed by the guide.

Kalanie is an old Buddhist town fourteen miles distant from Colombo, reached by a narrow road cut through a jungle of luxuriant growth. On the outskirts of the town we passed through several native settlements, meeting numerous venders carrying large baskets of the green betel-nut on their heads. From the size of the baskets and quantity of leaves one would imagine the supply coming into Colombo in the morning would be sufficient for the entire East; but they assured us not a single leaf would remain unsold by the evening. We passed crowds of children playing in the narrow streets, where vegetables and fresh fruits are sold on the side-walk by half-clad and wretched natives. We could not drive very fast for fear of running over the small urchins squatting about the roadway, enjoying to their heart's content a game of marbles, played just as children would in our country.

Here and there was a pretty Buddhist home; and sometimes the devout inmates were tracing white arabesque designs in chalk on the hard, yellow ground before their doors, placing at each end of the lines bunches of the roses of Sharon, red and brilliant against the sun-baked earth, — it being the Singalese way of honoring a saint's fête. In their

Tengyur, Buddhists have particular directions laid down for constructing magical squares and angles around the images of tutelary saints who are thus worshipped. Such figures are varied according to the school of the disciple: some patterns are rounded, some oblong, others square; and traced in colored chalks, they resemble the decorative pavement-drawings used for advertisements in cities.

Farther on a river is crossed by a bridge of boats which earned a title for the architect. The narrow stream is bordered and shaded by thickets of cocoanut-palms which Mark Twain describes as "feather-dusters struck by lightning." I fancy this comes from the slanting angle of their slender trunks, ending in a tuft of feathery leaves, which gives the whole country the effect of having been swept by a hurricane. Ten of these cocoanut-trees are a native's wedding portion to his daughter,—a valuable heritage indeed, when you consider the great possibilities of usefulness to a native household. The Singalese rely solely on the leaves for thatching their huts; avail themselves of the juice, called *tody*, for convivial occasions; make the fibre into cloth; to say nothing of the cocoanuts themselves, which furnish them milk and capital curry.

At last we reached the jungle. Ever since I had been in this country I had been pining to see a tropical jungle,—a real haunt of wild animals and deadly snakes. On both sides of the road stretched a forest of thick, interminable, green palms and bananas, interwoven with vines and clinging plants. Here were the bread-fruit-trees and spreading mangoes, many rare ferns and fantastic bushes, besides the jack-tree, whose mammoth green fruit, shaped like a prickly gourd, runs tear-like down the trunk, instead of growing properly on branches in a conventional manner. It was all indescribably beautiful, and awed one by the intense, the absolute silence of desolation broken only by the bird dwellers of its dark and lonely depths. Nothing could induce a person, other than a native or a most enthusiastic sportsman, to venture ten feet in the tall stems of purple foliage or the green thicket of branching boughs. The vegetation is almost too luxuriant; it goes against man's efforts towards cultivation, as the Arctic barrenness would discourage one in this lack of vegetation. Everything grows so rank, — cut away a root, and flowers will cover the earth; a little twig stuck into the ground becomes a tree in a year.

I wish I could take some of the fascinating photographs one could so easily make. Every spot is a picture; and there are so many delicious places and queer scenes that a camera would be better than a volume of letters. Now and then we pass native huts, thatched down to the ground with cocoanut fibre, where, from the inky blackness of the only opening in the house, a native appears in his ragged waist-cloth, only less dark than his habitation. The only touch of color is the great yellow stem of bananas hanging in the doorway, cut fresh this morning from his own stock of trees in the jungle. These he may dispose of during the day for a couple of annas, should a passer-by have need of them.

The temples at Kalanie form a collection of rude and neglected shrines, dirty and ill-kept, but interesting as the oldest Buddhist remains in Ceylon. Kalanie was once a famous seat of Buddhist learning, and known all over the Eastern world. What a change, — almost all traces of former grandeur have vanished! The most ancient building is a kiln-shaped, white-plastered tope, its base half hidden by tall grasses. The interior remains a secret; no permission to visit the shrine has ever been extended to travellers. This tope is claimed by the monks to date with the pyramids; an antiquity very absurd and unfounded according to a recent statement of Max Müller, who places the earliest Vedic hymns about 1500 B.C., and declares that Buddhism stands to Brahminism as Protestanism stands to Roman Catholicism; and to effect such changes and reforms requires centuries. So the enormous antiquity of our Kalanie tope must be brought forward from the youth of the world into her more vigorous age. It has been truly said, "that Oriental scholarship has wrought an almost miraculous change among the ruins of the past. What was old has become new; what was young has become old."

Children, beautiful, dark-eyed children, offer us temple flowers, and, on seeing us arrive, cry, in a well-meant effort of welcome, "Good-by, lady! good-by." They are simply the most lovely children ever seen, with great dreamy eyes and bright expressive faces. They are a great deal prettier and more graceful than our village children, and came swarming around us, darting behind some shelter when warned by the priests in emphatic Singalese and gestures, which we could understand, at least that they must leave our ladyships in peace.

Two priests were being photographed by an amateur under a sacred bo-tree. We observe the mild brethren of the yellow robe, in spite of their perfectly impassive countenances expressing a would-be attainment of an earthly Nirvana, show that little touch of human vanity, in posing before the camera, which makes the whole world kin. One of the priests afterwards volunteered to show us the temples, where the life and work of Buddha was rudely pictured in bright colors on the walls. After a struggle to conquer English words, which I thought would cause his sudden death, the yellow priest, exhausted from his labors, drew a disconsolate breath, and pointing to the still unexplained pictures and sculptures of his master, Buddha, said: "Lady know repeat Edwin Arnold; lady know repeat everything," — which means that the "Light of Asia," containing Buddha's life-history, would relieve the poor monk of future efforts to enlighten us. It is a perfect enchantment to be here; the quiet Buddhist temple, the impassive priests, the roguish little fairies of children, and ourselves, — the heirs of all the ages, meeting in this distant, mysterious, and sacred place of the ancient religion. But the sun is getting high, and it is quite time we were starting for home.

December 31.

We left Colombo at seven, yesterday morning, for this mountain retreat of Kandy. The baggage consisted of our English boxes in the van, seven cushions, one quilted comforter, one lunch-basket, four large and two small bags, three heavy rugs, with numerous jackets and coats. Our destination is seventy-two miles from Colombo; but it must be acknowledged that each mile might fairly count for six American ones if the difficulty of getting over it were considered: so the journey occupied four hours of a beautiful morning, and the road climbed a succession of hills, and from the top of each opened a wide and lovely prospect.

We travelled in an open, airy, tropical railway-carriage, with cushioned seats around three sides of the compartment, without window-glass, and shaded from the sun's rays by an overhanging roof. This road was built, under great difficulties, to connect Colombo with the cool mountain heights of frosty Neuraellia; and Kandy is the first stage on the journey. It is difficult to imagine how this road could be built through the marshy country below the hills, — a perfect laboratory of fevers and other deadly enemies of mankind. Kandy is 1650 feet above mean sea-level; and the climate is several degrees cooler than on the coast.

It is holiday-time; and all the government officials of Colombo have run up to enjoy their Christmas sports, made possible by this cooler atmosphere. The ancient chiefs of Kandy had a rank and power among the greatest in the island. To-day there remains of the ancient kingdom but a souvenir of gray-bearded men. In the far distance one can discern on clear days a high, blue chain of mountains crowned with the well-known Adam's Peak. It seems that near the summit of the peak one finds in the rock a cavity which produces a very faithful effect of a gigantic human foot. This excavation is claimed by the Hindus, who recognize here the foot of Siva; the Buddhists, of Buddha; the Chinese, another patron saint; the Mahometans, Adam; and the Portuguese, I believe, very appropriately claim it for Doubting Thomas. To-day it is possessed by the Buddhists, who have raised there a little chapel, — a sacred place of pilgrimage.

CHAPTER V.

IN A SINGALESE PARADISE.

KANDY, New Year's Day.

JUST think of it, January first; the hot sun and flower-scented air of Kandy; and B. and I sitting on the piazza of this hotel in the thinnest of summer gowns! Perfection made perfect would faintly describe this Kandy, this supposed Parâdis Terestre, this actual garden of the whole earth. Yesterday afternoon we left for a drive about five o'clock. The walks and drives of Kandy wind through a jungle of primeval forest-palms and acacia-trees; their names are prettily chosen from the wives of the governors of the island, — Lady Gordon's walk, Lady Horton's walk, and so on. The dense shade of high, fringed palms and creepers border high and low the streak of red roadway through the endless green of the forest. Wild flowers are purple masses; creepers grown at home in hot-houses cover in wild luxuriance every hut and space in all directions. Vines grow larger than the tree trunks they encircle, and hang in a perfect shower of gorgeous red flowers. All our hot-house plants run perfectly wild over the country in greatest profusion. Such a spot! One must be silent, or fail in the attempt to describe the beautiful ferns and foliage growing in the damp, shady forest.

Later in the afternoon we re-enter the town, and pass some shops. The Kandian merchants are very anxious for the unwary traveller to enter their little traps, and most picturesque and persuasive they are in showing their delicate *repoussé* gold and silver work. In olden times, Kandian knives were among the most famous in the world. Few ancient specimens exist outside of the museum; but every shop contains clever imitations, buried in the earth for years, to obtain the ancient rust and mould. A white-turbaned Bombay merchant is selling these knives, exquisitely wrought and chased in silver. We are on the point of being tempted, but stop to listen to a warning story told us by our companion, an old tea-planter, several years in Ceylon. "Not many years ago," he says, "Mr. L——, from London, a well-known dealer in Eastern curios, stayed at Kandy. He was fascinated one day into bargaining for an old knife, a Kandian blade, said to be at least two thousand years old, belonging, the merchant declared, to his own great-grandfather, who had inherited it. While the bargain was going on, Mr. L—— took out his handkerchief and quietly commenced rubbing the

ROAD-MAKERS.

blade of the knife. The merchant went on bargaining, and Mr. L—— polishing the blade, until the original mark was shown; then he said to the astonished merchant: 'You say this belonged to your grandfather; did your grandfather live in Sheffield?'"

Unprogressive Kandy, you are so indescribably Eastern and inexpressibly queer, so slow in some respects to adopt new ideas, yet so willing in other ways to go on with the times! Fancy the scene I witnessed to-day from my balcony window. A number of coolies let down buckets into the lake opposite the hotel, filled them with water, and scattered in all directions over the town to sprinkle the dusty streets. The talk at dinner last evening ran on this same subject,—the unreadiness of the natives to adopt new customs; and for illustration, I listened to a story something like this: When the railroad was being made to Kandy, the laboring natives used a sort of prehistoric pick and shovel combined, to break the ground and take the dirt away at the same time. The work was so slow and wearisome for the coolies, that some humane contractor bought them wheelbarrows. Now, what do you think they did with these new and strange implements? Put them at once on their heads and carried them. From carrying their fruits and baskets on their heads, the natives have at least learned to walk superbly, and to hold themselves straight and well.

For many days it has not only been very warm in the sun, but a light hot air has blown over everything, not strong enough to be called a hot wind, yet it sometimes scorches like the breath from a furnace mouth. The heat at mid-day is something dreadful; but we are cautioned that the damp air of the evening will bring out any fever you may have lurking about you, so we rarely sit in the wind by night, and by day avoid the sun as we would the evil one. This Ceylon, with all its fascination of life and scenery, is but a gilded cage, well enough to visit and keep lovely memories of hereafter, but one would not live here to possess the rubies of its richest mountains. You cannot help feeling a genuine sympathy for these poor English younger sons, or struggling planters, who own plantations, and live in the midst of their coolies far away on the mountainous tea-estates; they all dislike the life, which means separation from family and country, and rush back to their cold and foggy England the very moment the golden way is wide enough for them to walk on it.

One of these tea-estates lies about four miles from the town, and it was there we drove this afternoon after four o'clock tea. Leaving Kandy, in a few minutes we were amid the tropical vegetation which makes a green and tangled girdle about the old town as far as the eye can reach. Plunging through the sandy roadway, our destination was reached in passing fields of reedy bamboos, cinchona-trees, and rustling broad-leaved bananas, to a clearing, where the tea-house stands, folded about by the rolling hills, planted with the sentinel-like bushes of the tea-plant. How green and fragrant and quiet it all is! Nothing could be a greater contrast to the bustling factory life of our country towns than this quiet scene, where soft-footed coolies move noiselessly about their various occupations of sorting, drying, and picking the tea-leaves, with as little bustle and clatter as so many dark, barefooted ghosts. The owner of this tea-estate is a Mr. A——, and it is called by the soft-sounding name of "Peradeniya." The tea was growing on small stubby bushes, about one or two feet from the ground; excepting a few months during the summer, it is picked the year round. Hundreds of dark-skinned natives go forth in the early morning, armed for the work with long reed baskets carried on their heads, — the men with a few yards of muslin fastened about the waist; the women brightly draped in cottons, falling gracefully from the shoulders to the bare knee, one end of the scarf thrown completely over the head. Bright bits of colored glass made into jewelry decorate the throat; and from feet and ankles, ears and nose, are looped circles of gold, more or less valuable, which are the women's pride of life. Even little children are pressed into the service,—solemn, little, sad-eyed children, stunted and overworked, as different as possible from the laughing and capering boys and girls of other lands.

The coolies pick only the first three or four leaves of the plant; the larger leaves make the coarse tea, the smaller and more tender ones the medium grades; and the delicious orange Pekoe is produced from the first leaf and the little yellow bud that grow at the ends of the stem. As each basket is filled, it is brought by the natives to the receiving-room of the tea-house and weighed, each one separately, and pay given to the coolie on the spot. It is difficult to imagine a more picturesque scene than these people present in their gay dresses, filing in through the doorways, and heaping up the great rich green of the tea-leaves in masses almost as tall as themselves. After the green leaves have been scattered on canvas frames to wither for a day and a half, the leaf is taken to fomenting vats, then dried in furnace heat and sifted, when the finest quality falls into one box, the coarser into another, which becomes Pekoe, the next grade, broken Pekoe and Souchong; afterwards, scraps, dust, and scrapings of the tea fall from the sifter. This is the tea which is considered by the first planters the best in the market, and is always used for their own tea-drinking; as one can easily see, it must be the very smallest and most delicate bud which passes through the finest grade of sifter. This tea-dust never comes to America, but is sometimes sold in England for a few pence a pound. The Ceylon brand is a cross from the Assam and Chinese, and has become the latest fad in England.

Leaving the tea-house after having a cup of the most delicious tea I ever tasted, we returned through the Peradeniya garden, which lies close to Kandy. Such a spot! The beauty cannot be exaggerated, for sun and soil have combined to make this garden the most luxuriant in the world. It is impossible to enumerate the beautiful and rare vegetation which it contains. From the entrance portals, tall and massive, and covered with a showery curtain of unfamiliar vines and creepers, stretch avenues of tropical palms and india-rubber-trees, whose enormous branches interlace, making a green archway above our heads, the roots spreading out like giant blades in serpentine coils about two feet high above the ground. The huge bamboos are magnificent, their trunks quite large enough to make a fair-sized bucket; and by the riverside the culms attain a height of one hundred feet; and once sprouted, sometimes grow several inches an hour. Here are the curious banyan-trees, whose branches span the roadside, and taking root spring up in great luxuriance, so as to outrival the parent tree; mangoes, like spreading oaks, loaded with the delicious fruit; the gamboge-tree of Ceylon, which contains the yellow color in its sap and bears fruit golden and juicy; and wild banana-trees, a single leaf from which would clothe a man from head to foot. In fact, the garden, and Kandy itself, are a sort of botanical Noah's Ark, where every plant is represented, from the tall talipot-palm, which bears majestic flowers once in fifty years and then dies, to the simple white jessamine of our Carolina hedges. Orchids flutter like bright-colored birds from the branches of the tall trees, and the air is oppressive with the scent of a hundred blossoms of the garden flowers. These are the public gardens of Ceylon, and are kept in order by the government officials.

I cannot leave this garden without speaking of the palms. Certainly, the great feature of Peradeniya is these graceful trees, growing in thickets and masses on every side whichever way you turn, and I should think of at least a hundred different varieties — not the fragile nurslings of our greenhouses, with their few precious leaves, to be guarded and cared for against cold or change of temperature; in this country palms grow as they might have grown in the garden of Eden, their massive leaves piled one against the other in dense profusion, making the graceful shade trees so often spoken of in Bible history. You could wander for acres and acres among the acacias and mangoes, but you can never get away from the palms of all descriptions, from the giant fig to the Florida palmetto. After seeing the gardens, there can no longer be any doubt in one's mind that Ceylon's claim to be the home of the "grand old gardener and his wife" is at least well founded, for certainly here "every prospect pleases," as Bishop Heber says; and the first man is, was, and ever will be, according to the English residents' opinion of the native man, "vile."

Nothing is more surprising on a first visit to the East than to see how little confidence Europeans put in the natives, and how extremely they dislike to trust them. In Ceylon, it seems that in the country the fruit would be much improved were it only left. Now, these European owners of banana-trees cut the fruit green and house it, for the horticultural natives would certainly steal the fruit should it remain on the trees to ripen, thereby depriving them of their income for a whole year. Every man steals from his neighbor, every village from the next, and every province from the one adjoining. In spite of this unfortunate trait in their characters, the natives are undoubtedly an intelligent people, good-natured and easy to influence; their laziness is their great draw-back, but that can be readily understood and con-doned after even a few weeks' acquaintance with the tropical sun. One of the queer customs in this country is that there is no hay made when the sun shines; or, in fact, at any other time, no hay and no harvesting. When a horse is to be fed, a native coolie goes out to a field or damp open place and pulls away at the grass; in fifteen minutes he has picked a large bunch of grass, roots, and dirt, which he makes up into a little bundle, and shaking out the loose earth, feeds to his horses. Paddy and gram form the oats of the Singalese horses. Paddy is the island name for rice, which grows in the wet terraces, and is almost the only food ever seen by the native population, except bananas, the natives' bread, the great universal staple, from the little thatched hut in the jungle to the governor's palace.

Kandy is situated at the foot of a circle of mountains, bathed by a little lake, where numerous pagodas are reflected with their heavy belt of palms. At the head of the lake stands the temple of the Buddhist monks, and ever since I have been here I have longed to visit it. To-night, just as the sun was setting blood-red over the rosy lake, I had my wished-for experience. You have only to walk across the bund, and you are there,—before a low, turreted building, gray and mossy, surrounded by a moat. This temple holds the precious relic of Buddha's tooth, and is the most sacred shrine of Buddhism west of China. At the head of the marble stairway sits a yellow priest, who receives annas from the faithful, while close by are men arranging flowers in baskets and bunches, to be presented to the idol. I found myself in a crowd of natives, of all types and conditions, waiting for the hour when the shrine would be open for the adoration of the people. Were it not for local color, one could easily imagine oneself before some Catholic sanctuary in Italy or France. Buddha having left no doctrine of the existence of God or of the soul, his disciples exalted their master to the place of a deity, showing that the natural instinct to worship something must be gratified, and proving the truth of the French saying, "If there were no God, it would be necessary to invent one." Having no Supreme Being in their religion, there is no need of a priesthood, — the intermediary between God and man, — so instead of the priest they have the monk. At six o'clock precisely, appears a procession of men, beating tomtoms and rattling cymbals, making a most ferocious racket, ushering in two of the yellow brethren, who open the massive carved door of the shrine, flanked by two reclining elephants; then, after unlocking another silver door, enter together with a crowd of natives, who press forward and peer through the bars which separate us from the silver table, where, under a jewelled bell, shining with precious stones, is the famous relic. You are dazzled by the rubies, sapphires, and true oriental cat's-eyes, imbedded in the golden covering. The tooth itself we were not permitted to see; but we were told that it was of such size that it would give you a very peculiar impression of its possessor, if it is not indeed, as many people think, borrowed from the mouth of a tiger or crocodile. The service seemed to consist in offerings of flowers, — the sweet blossoms of the temple flower, fragrant jessamines, and tulip buds. These fragrant gifts are cleared away every morning by attendant priests; but so faithful are the votaries to the shrine, that the place is never free from the sweet-scented masses of blossoms showered there in reckless profusion. After leaving, we peered about the marble galleries and corridors of the outer temple, seeing some wonderful carvings and grotesque paintings of the Buddhist Inferno. The different punishments meted out to bad Buddhists are frescoed in bright colors on the walls, as if fresh from the hand of the Italian artist of the Campo Santo at Pisa. For instance, the native who has offended the law in taking animal life, is pictured as a fish being hooked successively by gigantic fish-hooks, from each of which he releases himself only to fall back on a greater one. The intemperate Buddhist is most amusingly represented as receiving his punishment in a more cruel manner than Tantalus himself. The fresco shows a man stretched out on a fiery bed, while an imp hovers over him with a cooling drink, just out of reach of his parched lips. Other tortures are more cruelly imagined than those of Greek mythology, where men and women most painfully ascend ladders of swords, and so on. The visit that I treasure most in my memory was to an upper room of the temple, which is used by the Buddhists as a library. Finding several priests writing in the room, we hesitated to enter; but through our guide were cordially pressed to do so with true Eastern hospitality. I can never describe the impression made by these Buddhist monks, so calm and impassive, unearthlike they seem, — the very living example of the lines in which Edwin Arnold describes them, in the "Light of Asia." "Feeds his sense

> "No longer on false shows, files his firm mind
> To seek not, strive not, wrong not; bearing meek
> All ills which flow from foregone wrongfulness,
> And so constraining passions that they die."

The room was lined with cases containing books in many languages; among others, well-known English works and several American magazines, which they told us through our interpreter were immensely appreciated by the brotherhood. In one bookcase, behind the glass, are the dried leaves which Edwin Arnold gathered from the sacred ground at Buddha Gya, from the very bo-tree where the great master accomplished his great meditation. These were pointed out to us with great pride by the Buddhists, who afterwards told us that the "Light of Asla" had been translated into their language, and is considered a great book in all the East. This gave me an idea; and I immediately despatched a little native girl to the temple garden, to pick some leaves from the sacred bo-tree, on which I reverently asked the high-priest to write his names and titles, — a charming souvenir of the visit to the Buddhist sanctum.

The most precious possessions in the library were curious books of their ancient religion, written on the dry leaves of the talipot-palm, and bound together with silver covers exquisitely wrought and encrusted with costly jewels. I should not think that an intimate acquaintance with the books of that great library would be consistent with the Buddhist theory of life, which seems to consist principally in contemplating oneself and seeking charity. The most common sight in Kandy is a Buddhist monk, standing with downcast eyes at the doorway of a native, accompanied by a little novice, who carries his umbrella. A wooden bowl is hidden under the folds of his gown, to be replenished with the food which is cooked every morning and set apart for the use of the priests, who are forbidden to ask for it, but go silently from house to house, often waiting on the street for hours before they are observed and the food doled out to them.

I have acquired some knowledge of the duties and curious ceremonials of the *religieux* from a review of the Buddhist treatises contained in the library of the Secretary of State for India. In the Dulwa, or Discipline, are set forth the rules of life of the Indian *bhikshu* and *bhikshum*,—the male and female beggars of virtue. Several volumes are filled with the descriptions of the offences which a beggar may commit, and with commands forbidding the use of garlic, and giving the proper style of garment,—without sleeves, and of yellow muslin. No ordinance exists against the smaller vanities. Rings of copper, ivory, or brass are allowed; but gold rings are tabooed, which suggest that the rules are aimed principally against extravagance. According to the Dulwa, umbrellas must be relegated to a dim antiquity. A positive direction is laid down, which allows to the monks two,—one to guard against the rain, the other against the sun. A German writer has given us some new thoughts concerning the parallel which Sir Edwin Arnold attempts to draw between the life of Christ and the career of Buddha. He makes it quite clear that there is no analogy in the leading occurrences of the two lives. One leads an active life of practical charity; the other, an inactive, meditative existence,—doing nothing for the mere temporal relief of his fellow-creatures, believing all earthly comfort and help to be illusions. The date of Buddha's career and the year fixed by different historians of his death differ as widely as the causes assigned to his taking-off. A Thibetian narrative ascribes his decease to a spinal malady, but the Singalese disciples believe he died from making an excessive meal of pork.

COLOMBO, January 5.

In Colombo once more. It is like coming home. Our old friends, the Mahometan shopkeepers, invite us in by name when we pass their shops. The jinrikisha coolies crowd around with their funny little conveyances, which look like overgrown baby-carriages, ready to carry us in any direction for the very moderate compensation of half a rupee (twenty cents) per hour; or we might choose a bullock-cart, — one bullock, ten cents an hour; while still another vehicle awaits our pleasure, a Singalese palanquin, — an open coach, with turbaned outriders and the usual barefooted runners who clear the way. Indeed, I have scarcely seen a shoe or stocking in Ceylon. We have had a long shore breeze to-day, enchanting enough if one could only enjoy it; but five minutes' exposure to this fatal wind would have an almost disastrous effect. These are the fascinating hours, between five and six, when all Ceylon takes itself off to Galle Face, to enjoy the refreshing glimpse of the ocean; and we also decide to walk out on this glorious promenade, and take one last view of the dear Indian Ocean. We meet many gayly-painted palanquins, and catch glimpses of the wives of the native grandees inside, who wear low-necked gowns, driving or walking, — a very sensible custom in this climate, for the thermometer in Ceylon averages about seventy-six the year round; the hot season being January, February, and March, which is just the reverse of what we are accustomed to expect. Distant only three and a half degrees from the equator, the days and nights are almost of equal length, and night falls with scarcely a warning, like a great black curtain rung down on a scene in the theatre, and the stars come out bright, and shine as they only can in the clear Eastern atmosphere. From Galle Face the sea breaks for miles on the coral reefs, the foam is tossed off of emerald waves for miles on the red sand of the beach. The sky takes that peculiar amber hue which comes before a fine sunset, and the sun itself spreads long parting flashes of golden light over earth and sea; and over all the spell, the glow of the coming Indian night.

CHAPTER VI.

BOMBAY.

INDIAN OCEAN, EN ROUTE FOR BOMBAY.
P. and O. Steamer "Thames," January 11.

WE are still in the tropics, but the sea-air is refreshing after the glare of sand and torrid heat in Ceylon. The water is smooth, and does not by any means show its stormy character. We are skirting close to the Western Ghauts, low, brown and yellowish in color, and dotted with stubby green trees. These Ghauts form a natural wall of defence running along the entire coast from Bombay to Cape Comorin; and we keep them well in sight from the long, low sea-chairs, drawn close to the water-side under the awning, where we spend our days. The passengers are the usual English officers, with a sprinkling of tourists. Far more interesting are the Orientals, in the second cabin, the dark Africans, or Bombay merchants, draped in thin white muslin and high turbans: there are also several Parsee men and women on board, who occupy one side of the forward deck, and are left quite to themselves by general consent. They bring their own servants and provisions; and as you make a circuit of the ship, you are sure to catch a whiff of disagreeable odors, which makes you turn quickly from their vicinity. Here they sit all day, huddled together among smoking dishes of unsavory food, or asleep on rugs in the midst of cackling chickens and bleating sheep, which their cooks will prepare for the next day's meal. The Parsee women are as small and dainty as the Chinese, and wear loose, bright-green and gold *saris*,[1] draped to cover them from the head to the little feet in one single piece.

We land at five o'clock to-day. A little tug steams up the great harbor, through lines of war-ships and merchant-vessels of all nations, landing our passengers and the royal mail at the Apollo Bunder; the voyage has been so smooth that it scarcely seems that we have changed one element for another. We take a gharri to the Esplanade Hotel,—a high brown caravansary, with many verandas, looking across the large open square encircled by great public buildings and government offices, which remind you very much of an English city. The streets are irregular, but of splendid dimensions, bordered with tall houses, each one differing from the other in style and color, the ground-floor forming the shops, in which one may find specimens of every style of merchandise

[1] *Sari*, a sheet-like, native drapery, of silk or muslin.

in the East. The busy life, however, of the busiest city at home can scarcely imitate the turbulent waves of various nationalities, the bustling crowds of this Oriental city. Through these streets sweep a variety of types and races, which outrival in color and brilliancy anything of the kind in the East. Here and there, a European in civilized clothes may be seen, who soon disappears in the ocean of color, which seems as if the kaleidoscope had been broken by some giant hand, and the colors scattered over everything. There are as many shades of color in complexion as in costume, — Mahometans, with enormous turbans of green or white, and long beards dyed a brilliant red, as a proof that they have made the pilgrimage to Mecca; rich Chinese, in gorgeously embroidered pantaloons and long black cues, with silk vests under white silk redingotes, their pleated umbrellas inevitably raised above the head; Parsees, all in white, with high, funnel-shaped hats, spangled with black and gold, which recede in the back, forming a sort of hollow, in which is placed an indoor cap of velvet or satin. Above this throng, a Yogi stands rigid on the steps of the Hindu temple, gaunt, thin, and immovable, — his stiffened limbs, thin, naked, and covered with ashes; his long hair, matted together with ropes, hangs straight to his waist. Long jungle-hardships have so weakened the intellect, torture, suffering, and penance have so long been his fate, that I think this would-be holy man is almost an imbecile; but so worshipped and reverenced by the Hindus that they crowd about him to mark their faces with the ashes which cover his flesh, with as much devotion as the penitents of Ash-Wednesday in Catholic countries.

The native dwellings are in separate parts of the town. The Mahometan quarter is quite distinct from the Hindu, as the latter is from the Parsee. All that part of Bombay bordering on the water is called The Fort, where are situated public edifices, government offices, the cottages and churches — not differing very greatly from any other finely laid out city. At one extremity rises a wooded hill, and here are the bungalows of nearly all of the official population. Here too are the flower-terraced gardens of the Parsees, that strange Eastern sect of fire-worshippers, who came hither many years ago from Persia.

The Parsees are the Jews of Bombay, its richest merchants, its greatest bankers, most honored citizens. Like the Hebrews, they are generous and charitable, and a beggar among them is entirely unknown. Many of them have amassed colossal fortunes; and, it must be confessed, have employed them to the benefit of the entire population of Bombay, — Hindus and Europeans, as well as their own people. Several Parsees have been knighted as a reward for their immense charity. Sir Jamsetji Jijibhoi is called the benefactor of his people, his charities amounting to thousands of rupees,—having built a hospital, museums, roads, and endowed colleges, etc., during the last fifteen years. The Parsees are immensely patriotic, are considered the best subjects that Queen Victoria has in India, and many have passed through Oxford and Cambridge in as good shape as the native-born Englishmen. They worship fire in their temples, and are said to keep the flame alive by constantly supplying it with precious essences. We were not allowed to enter their temples, which are never profaned by unbelieving travellers, it being almost an impossibility to procure a permit. The Zoroastrians never smoke, because it would be such utter wickedness to put out the fire of even the smallest cigarette; and they employ special Hindu servants to extinguish the lamps in their houses. They also reverence greatly all the elements, but, above all, the sun; although I fancy a Parsee graduate of Oxford would be highly indignant at being dubbed a sun-worshipper: still he would probably admit that his Bombay brothers adore the sun in their prayers as being the highest manifestation of the greatness of the Supreme God visible to our human sight.

In the afternoons the drives on Malabar Hill are lined with Europeans and natives walking, driving, and sitting about the gardens of roses under the high, flowering trees, which border the roadway, and overlook the great stretch of sea, and the sunlit waters of the beautiful Bay of Bombay. The residents drive in beautiful carriages, with footmen in gorgeous Eastern liveries; and we add our due share of color to the scene with a luxurious open barouche, two men on the box in green turbans, — fifty yards of fine silk in each, — white jackets, and trousers to the bare knee, black legs and feet, gold and green sashes about their waists, and two more of these extraordinary natives standing behind and continually dismounting to clear the way for our carriage to pass. Lord Harris, the governor of Bombay, and many others, dash by us in similar carriages, with postilions gorgeously arrayed in red and gold silk turbans, brilliant coats covered with tinsel, and sashes of gold lace, and, honesty bids me say, minus the stocking and shoe, their brown legs contrasting curiously with the bright red and gold of the livery. The feature of this scene, the dazzling Eastern part of it, is when the sun is sinking in tropical splendor far out over the golden path it makes from land to sea. Then the Parsee women alight from their carriages, and in their saris of pale lemon, rosy pink, and faintest green, group about the palm-trees, and lifting up their hands, say their evening prayer to the setting sun, looking like a rainbow broken up in rays of color all over the palmy paths and ferny nooks of the hillside. Farther down toward the water's edge stand some venerable Parsees, with hands open before their faces, and heads bowed down even to the earth, repeating in the unknown language of the Zend Avesta the prayer of adoration, — the vesper hymn to the "Light that lighteth every man."

Before we leave Malabar Hill, scarcely a mile from the gay scene of the pleasure-loving people, the drive continues toward the Parsee place of sepulchre. Passing through the bordered driveway, we reach in half an hour two yellow-and-white gates, and are within the grounds of the "Towers of Silence." At the end of a flight of granite steps stretch acres of trees, flowers, and clusters of the climbing purple Borgan Villia in bright branches over the fresh young grass. The Parsees have surrounded this grewsome abode of death with every charm of natural beauty, to dispel as far as possible the gloomy impression made by this manner of disposing of their dead. A peculiarity of this religion is, that they never burn or bury their dead, but transport them to this place after death, stretched on iron slats and covered with white. Half hidden in different places among the trees you find the five white circular towers, and from the flowery terraces where we stand we can see the vultures perched in the turrets as thick as they can crowd together. Other cadaverous birds hover about the trees near by, and suddenly swoop down towards the towers; for they have scented a funeral approaching. From our place we see four priestly men, in loose white gowns and tall white Parsee hats, winding down the path. They carry a white-covered form, stretched on an iron rack; next, two men appear, — they are the mourners, — and then two more, all in the white loose gowns and white sashes, each couple carrying between them a handkerchief, — symbol of sympathy. About thirty yards from the tower they stop. The priests advance alone up an incline, open a door, and place the form of the dead one on the iron vaulting inside; when in a moment more the vultures descend, and in a half-hour nothing remains but the bare skeleton: another forty-eight hours, and the priests enter again, and by their sacred hands alone the bones are gathered up and placed in a well in the centre of the tower. This well is intended to hold the remains until they return to the dust and are led through a filter of stones to the earth. In this way the elements are never polluted, which would be a high sin in their eyes. No Parsee woman ever goes to the burial-place until her last journey. The funeral procession is formed solely of the men, and is always taken on foot. After the ceremony, and before leaving the grounds, every vestige of clothing worn at the burial is washed, and the mourners bathe in a large tank, replacing their funeral clothes of white by their ordinary garments. Even the priests bathe and remove their clothes before officiating at another ceremony, should it take place the next hour. An enchanting drive home, but the gloom of this terrible place is not easily dispelled.

At the commencement of January the temperature of Bombay mounts quite high enough to unfit a traveller to enjoy sight-seeing, but does not seem to unfit the residents from enjoying an immense amount of gayety. Tuesday evening we dined with an American friend at the Royal Yacht Club, and after dinner had an opportunity of attending a ball. The yacht club is charmingly situated on the bay. The green lawns in front of the buildings extend to the very borders of the ocean, where the fleet of boats are at anchor. The ball began at ten, and only ended in the morning hours. The company were principally Europeans in uniforms, with their wives and daughters in French ball-dresses, who danced with all the vivacity possible. It only takes a few years of this trying climate, however, to change the ruddiest English beauty into a pale-complexioned Anglo-Indian. There was scarcely a woman present who had the slightest claim to good looks. From the governor down to the lowest commissioned officer, they strive to drown their *heimweh* (homesickness), — to forget themselves in an incessant whirl of pleasure.

The suburbs of Bombay are lovely. Byculla is one, and also Matheran, which is situated a few hours from the capital, so that it can scarcely be called a suburb, but is a great resort for the people of Bombay in the hot season. That it is popular among other tribes than Europeans, I am no longer in any doubt, from the following, taken from a Bombay newspaper.

"COURTING AT MATHERAN. — A correspondent writing to a Bombay contemporary says: 'Matheran is supposed to swarm with honeymooning couples; but we never could find any, though we looked for a little amusement in this way, and we began to think that in this respect also, Matheran was a delusion and a snare. But at last we found an ideal pair. They had apparently been having a little quarrel, — or, perhaps, only a misunderstanding. Edwin was at some distance from Angelina, regarding her moodily, while she was pensively surveying the scenery. Both seemed as if they would make it up, but each was too proud to take the initiative. We watched them attentively. At last Edwin evidently came to the conclusion that things had gone far enough; and he edged gently towards his better half, while Angelina had her eye upon him, though she coyly pretended not to see him. It was really as good as a play. Finally, Edwin stood quite close beside Angelina, and put his hand on her shoulder. Then her pride gave way, and she turned round, and they gave each other such a hug that it was most touching to see them. Suddenly something startled them, and with a bound they were on the top of a tree chattering profusely. They were the finest pair of Matheran apes that we saw on the hill. Anything more human could not have been imagined. We no longer doubt the truth of Darwin's theory.'"

I have had many pleasant entertainments in my life, but never a pleasanter one than on the afternoon I spent with Mrs. H., of the Presbyterian Mission at Bombay, among her own little Hindu and Mahometan school children, who had invited us to a native feast. I never saw children so happy and bright as these little women; they laughed and chattered together like so many magpies. All the little girls wore the Indian sari, — about nine yards of bright cotton cloth, pleated about the waist, with one end thrown over the shoulder and head. This was a great fête-day; and the little women had been impatiently looking forward to it as the one fixed to receive the contents of boxes sent from America to the mission children, which did not come on Christmas, and so were to be distributed on this day, — the end of the school year. About fifty little women were learning wisdom in Mrs. H.'s mission school. The gray stone building was opened on all sides by arches, to let in the sweet air from the

KOOLIN BRAHMINS.

gardens; and as we entered, the little girls all rose at the same time, pointed their pretty hands before their faces, bent low, and called sweetly to us, *Namouska,* — greeting. B. and I were made proud and happy by being accommodated with seats at the head of the room with Mrs. H. and other friends, and exactly opposite to us were lifted the expectant faces. Some of the little girls are not more than three or four years old; and yet, according to native custom, they are already betrothed, and wear nose-rings of gold, and ear-rings of precious stones looped in heavy circles around the entire rim of the ear, and their feet are loaded with bangles. Many have anklets of silver balls, which are perfect torture to their possessor. Grave and learned pundits are engaged in grafting English and Sanscrit, besides various other roots and branches, on the minds of the children, which seems a very rational employment in this country of premature intelligence and industry.

What an inevitable destroyer of caste is a native school! Mrs. H. points out to us a Coolin Brahmin girl, who is sitting next a low-caste Banniah, in utter disregard of the iron laws of the Brahmins. After a great struggle, Mrs. H. has taught the natives to sing hymns in English. Their idea of music differs from ours in many ways. There is no second part in their songs, which consist in reality of a few notes, sung in monotonous time and measure. When the hymns were ended, each little one came up with great gravity of expression when her name was called, to receive a gift, returning to her bench with beaming eyes, hugging to her heart the staring, blue-eyed, tow-haired dolly, as great a contrast as possible to the little dark-skinned child. The festival over, we drove to a large columned bungalow near by, surrounded by beautiful mango-trees, which is the latest purchase of the Mission Board. About thirty girls live here in native fashion quite by themselves; and here the feast was to take place. On the gray stone floor of the principal room, Arabesque lines were chalked in colors, which served to designate the place of each guest; and before these squares were placed a fresh banana leaf and a brass drinking-cup, the only table service that we could discover.

But first I must tell you that there were no chairs or benches, and no choice was left us but to squat on our heels in the native fashion. It was hard to be dignified on this occasion and in this position, and we rolled over on our backs several times in our efforts to keep our bodies upright. The little Hindus were convulsed, but politely concealed their amusement; no doubt, however, they were laughing at us in their sleeves. On the banana leaf were spread little heaps of different vegetables, cooked with spices and chutneys and chillies and peppers. A banana stew looked at least tempting before we tasted it, but it was cooked with so much red pepper that we could scarcely swallow it. There were no forks, knives, or spoons; and nothing would do but we must manage to partake of the food with our fingers in the native manner. Of course we failed. The little Hindus simply beamed with delight, and offered to show us how easily they could do it, — by just pressing the food in a little ball with two fingers, and with the other three sweep up the sauce which covers the leaf, and gracefully convey it to their mouths, without spilling a single drop and scarcely soiling their fingers. They were delighted to hover about and wait on us, but would have broken caste had they eaten even the smallest grain of rice.

The banana leaf is used instead of crockery, according to the Hindu idea of cleanliness, as it can be destroyed every morning, and never used a second time. The cooking utensils are all of brass, scoured and cleaned to a point never reached by civilized people. No glass or china is ever used; the drinking-cups and platters, which cost almost nothing, and eliminate the item of breakage in household expenditures, serve for general family use.

After the feast, we all had seats in the big square court of the house, and the children played for us their native games. Anything more graceful cannot be imagined, and the amount of spirit they put into these fantastic romps outrivals anything I ever knew. A favorite amusement is the childish play of choosing a bride, — a real imitation of the ceremony as it is done in the East. A party of the older girls advance up the room, with the little bride that is to be, hidden behind their draperies. These represent the bride's relatives, and they are taking the little baby-girl to the house of the bridegroom. The bridegroom's friends are represented by taller girls, drawn up in line to receive them. As the bride's little party approach, they all sing the praises of their child in the flowery speech of the Orient. The rhyming words fall softly from sweet lips, and the eyes beam with laughter and fun. What they chant is something like this: "This is our daughter, the fairest among women, the pearl of the East; the lotus-eyed, the pride, the jewel of our life." At the end of this song, the bridegroom's friends answer in their turn: "Our boy is as glorious as the sun at evening, as brave as a rajput, as wise as a serpent." When they pause, it is the turn of the bride's relatives, who describe in still more glowing language the perfection and fascinations of their little one. This is answered again by the other side, who chant the praises of the bridegroom: "The son of a rajah, the possessor of herds and fine houses and lands, the joy of the household, the pride of his line." This exhausted, the two families come down to business. The bride's friends say, "Well, how much will you offer for this girl?" and if the groom's attendants do not put down sufficient inducement, or raise from their first offer to suit the demands of the girl's friends, the transaction is incomplete, and the little bride returns. All this time she has not been seen by the bridegroom's party, who are puzzled on these occasions to know just how far to trust the praises bestowed on her. After this follows a general frolic, where the children float and flutter, holding one another by the hand, whizzing through the air like small human tops, faster and faster still, until your eye can scarcely follow their graceful motions.

Later on, we went into the gardens to visit other buildings, where the girls cook for themselves, grind daily the corn used by the mission household at a stone mill, where they sit and sing and work for hours. Then we were shown the sleeping apartment, a long stone room, uncarpeted, and without an article of furniture. The only bed was a bamboo mat, placed by the side of the wall, with a gray woollen blanket rolled at the foot. Thirty of these rolls are placed in rows down the room. The girls in the mission school have no pillows, no sheets, nor anything more comfortable than this native bed. They have only had blankets since Christmas, when a small donation which came from America was appropriated by Mrs. H. to buy them. There are no closets for the wardrobes, but very recently wooden chests have been given them. Before this, they possessed no receptacle for clothing of any sort.

Indian twilights are short. It is growing dark, and we must leave Byculla and the mission, returning through three miles of lighted streets to our hotel. No one must fail to visit the curious animal hospital in Bombay, which has grown out of the religious veneration of animal life. I do not think one could form any idea before visiting the place just what an animal hospital would be like. This one, at least, is not like anything else in the world. Stopping before a gateway, we leave our horses to munch the fresh grass and corn-leaves, which the Hindu doorkeeper offers; and passing through the doorway, we find ourselves in the wards, which cover acres of ground, tenanted by sick animals, including every species from a cat to a camel. What a curious sight it is! — the cattle with every form of disease, some lying and some standing about the open wards, which form four sides of an open courtway. Farther on are the lame, halt, and blind of the poultry-yard; chickens, with one wing disabled, vanquished in a barnyard quarrel; pariah puppies, that had been picked up in the street in all stages of starvation or degradation; all manner of quadrupeds, some now on three legs, and others unable to stand at all; flocks of monkeys, who affect a sudden terror at your approach; and cages

A MISSION-SCHOOL GIRL.

of pigeons, parrots, and ailing birds of every description. All this is supported by the voluntary offerings of the Hindus, whose physicians make regular visits to the patients every morning. It is considered the greatest act of merit to leave a bequest to the animal hospital, which has become immensely rich from the thank-offerings of grateful Hindus. Our examination of the sick wards was far from microscopic, and it was necessary to summon all our courage to go as far as we did. The air you breathe at the hospital is foul to a degree which would make an abattoir seem pure by contrast. In fact, I think one is apt to sentimentalize too much over the Hindu hospital. It is a question whether it would not be much more merciful to the animals to despatch them at once rather than to keep them lingering on in a disabled, unhappy condition, when in most cases a cure is impossible.

The Hindus, of course, never eat animal food. To do this would be to go against their religion and their conscience, for in another life their respected grandfather may have become a plump duck or a tender chicken, which would make things very awkward. In one of the Indian provinces, near the Bombay Presidency, it is impossible for Europeans to buy lamb. The rajah's father died, and the Hindu high-caste Brahmin, whom the prince consulted, told him that his father had become a sheep after his soul had passed to the land of the dead. At once, the rajah sent forth an edict to the Europeans and Mahometans, which forbade the killing of the lambs of the flock forever.

One must be off early in the morning if one wishes to see the very prettiest sight in Bombay. About a mile from the town is the fine new building, with towers at the four corners, surrounded by lovely gardens, — the Flower Market. Inside, are long vistas of high piled-up fruit and vegetables, — great tropical fruits, mangoes, yellow and juicy, pink and white mangosteens, pomegranates, and guavas. Mammoth fruits, with unknown names, frame the little Hindu venders squatting among their wares in rows high above your head, and filling banana leaves with the fruit and vegetables, which they toss down from their high perch into the open arms of a little native housewife, who is selecting her day's supply. All the air of the gardens outside seems to be full of twittering, and I found the tall acacia-trees filled with bird-cages, tenanted by love-birds and paroquets, while near by were hundreds of little monkeys, caged, or swinging from the limbs of trees. Two cockatoos, in white and gold feathers, slip down from their perch and proceed to fight. The contents of the cages scream wildly; all their friends, the monkeys, chatter or howl in sympathy, and the insect life of the gardens buzzes and hums a minor accompaniment. The tree-birds chirp and twitter in every tongue known to bird life; and above the uproar rise the voices of the excited natives, adding to, instead of quelling, this babel of languages. It was the Hindu New Year's day, the great feast of the year. Nearly every one we met was in holiday dress. The saris of the women were even more brightly decorated than usual with gold tinsel and embroidery of yellow, green, or Indian-red, wearing about their necks long wreaths of the golden chrysanthemum-like flowers, which the women sell to the passers-by to honor the New Year.

The Esplanade Hotel, at which we are stopping, is large and roomy, but positively like barracks. One must indeed learn to do without luxurious surroundings during a trip to India. There are no carpets anywhere to be seen, and our bedrooms are furnished with severe simplicity. The bed is without springs, with a couple of quilted arrangements thrown over the bare slats; and I have not seen anything that resembled a table in my room, unless it is a wooden bench slatted like a chicken-coop. A bath-room, the necessity of life in India, is attached to each room, which is really the only comfort. You will look in vain for bells, electric or the opposite. Each room opens on a long balcony, and a call down several stories will soon bring a native *beastie*, or water-carrier, from the courtyard, carrying under his arm a buffalo skin, sewn together to contain water, the neck of the beast serving as a spout; and with this primitive arrangement, he fills your bath for the morning dip. A draught of air is as indispensable to the people in the East as it is dreaded by us at home. In the public buildings as in private houses, in the sleeping-rooms as well as in the salons, over the pulpit of the preacher as well as over the desk of the clerk, in fact everywhere, long pieces of canvas are suspended, attached to the ceiling by cords, which are pulled to and fro by a native, giving a delicious little breeze over our heads. These are the punkahs, and they are generally manipulated by a small specimen of Asiatic humanity, who is called a punkah-wallah. You often see one of these small boys fast asleep in the mid-day sun, with the punkah cord fastened to his great toe, — sleeping away blissfully, keeping up the action of the punkah from force of habit. The strangest system of lights is in use. Unless in the character of an outraged European you storm the office citadel, the only lumination you will ever see at night when you arrive at your number in the hotel, is a glass tumbler beside the door, filled with cocoanut oil, in which is floating a small lighted taper. We have at table a strange variety of food, and very badly cooked. The milk is from the buffalo cow, blue white and never creamy.

The butter is also white and very tasteless, but the fruit is abundant and delicious. We are served with five meals every day, including afternoon tea on the balconies, while we are reclining in long bamboo chairs, which look so comfortable and easy that they simply invite you to sit in them; for all this we pay five or six rupees a day, the average price for rooms and board at all the hotels in the East.

The wives of the common people in India show themselves in the streets unveiled, whether they be Mahometans or Hindus. It is only the higher classes who impose on their wives the seclusion of the harem. The women are generally dressed in striking colors, with silver rings and bangles from the wrist to the elbow. Mahometan women wear as a nose-decoration a flat gold stud, the sign of marriage. Brahmins and other Hindus have their noses pierced by circles of gold, some as long as a necklace, others so small that it would seem to cause them great embarrassment in taking their food. I have seen earrings of gold, spool-shaped, and heavily ornamented with stones, thrust through the lobe of the ear, which has been gradually pressed and flattened from childhood to receive this ornament. The cheapness of printed cottons from Manchester is bringing about the disappearance of hand-embroidered stuffs, which in olden times the Indian women wore universally. Why cannot the women of India keep forever this picturesqueness, — always wear this enchanting sari? Why lose the grace and charm of Eastern warp and woof, to adopt a costume destructive of all poetry, just because machines from Manchester have invaded fairy-land? Unfortunately, we have to learn that nations are not easily stopped, when once started on the road to public good by selfish notions of picturesque fitness which we, who so eagerly embrace every new and civilized comfort in dress or machinery, may strive to impose on them. As Browning says, —

> "But mankind are not pieces — there 's the fault;
> You cannot push them, and the first move made,
> Lean back and study what the next shall be,
> In confidence that when 't is fixed upon
> You find just where you left them, blacks and whites;
> Men go on moving when your hand 's away."

Nothing can be more irrational and uncivilized than the way mothers carry their children in this country, — the little ones astride their mothers' hips, held securely in this position by a firm arm about them. It is very shocking to see a fragile little mother, ten or eleven years old, her slight form bent out of shape under the weight of a bouncing baby half as large as herself. The native girls are betrothed when about three years old, and are almost universally married when from eight to ten years of age. But this is a common street sight that you are likely to see, wherever you turn. In the Indian women, especially among the lower castes, no robustness exists, no hearty vigor. They are undersized, undeveloped, and overworked, sentenced by their religion to have three masters, — their father, elder brother, and husband.

CHAPTER VII.

ALLAHABAD.

January 22.

LEAVING Bombay at ten o'clock P. M., on the Calcutta mail-train, we passed directly over the high Ghauts, and for two days and one night traversed the table-land of India. Indian railway carriages have a wide seat on each side of the compartment. At night, an extra berth is let down from above, on which you place your own pillows and *resai*,[1] draw the curtain over the night-lamp, and no one disturbs your slumbers by screaming the different stations or demanding tickets. All this time the ,train goes along leisurely twenty miles an hour, stops thirty minutes for chota-hazri, stops again for dinner, and then for afternoon tea, taken at dainty tables spread under vine-covered arbors and flowery trees. The Indian stations are the prettiest in the world, the station-master being stimulated by a prize offered yearly by the railway company for the most beautiful grounds and surroundings; the natives fill every space with flowers and shrubbery,

[1] *Resai*, an Indian blanket, wadded, and generally made of bright cottons.

WOMEN CARRYING WATER.

and plant vines to creep over the buildings themselves. Up and down the station paces the *bhistie* (water-carrier), who supplies water in brass lotas to thirsty travellers, replenishing his pouch, the tanned hide of a bullock, at the station well. They tell us this functionary is always a Brahmin, in order that the Hindus may drink the water safely without breaking caste; and should a low-caste person desire to quench his thirst, he must be content to have the water poured into his hollowed hand.

As a rule, the natives manage the iron roads, are the engineers, the trainmen, station babus, and fill no end of positions. Dozens and half-dozens rush towards an advancing train, scrutinize the occupants of the carriages, offer sticky sweetened balls of unknown ingredients, or steaming chai from thick white cups, with coarse sugar, and invariably oranges and bananas, with which we supply our lunch-basket, made of rattan from prudential motives. Our boxes now number thirteen pieces, and we have in addition a native servant, who is called in this part of India a "bearer." "Shanker," which you must pronounce "Shunker," is a Surati man, as we have found out to our sorrow. In Calcutta, the Bengali house-steward paid no heed to "Shanker's" request for soup, peas, or oranges, in compliance with our needs at table; and the dinner was usually prolonged at least a half-hour, all owing to his being of a lower caste and a different worship. It would seem the ideal way to have a new servant for each place, and of the religion prevailing in the country. It may seem queer to us that any people should trouble themselves over mixing up creeds and potatoes, or piety and pineapples, but one cannot conceive of the way these Eastern races live out their religious principles in every act of the day. Eastern servants require any amount of looking after; they require to be told the same thing over and over every day, and what is worse, besides telling, you must stand over them and see that they do it. You must also inform them by fragments just what you want of them, as they can't take in much at one time; but, after all, it is such a comfort to have some one always willing to do everything as a matter of course, having no other idea than that of serving you.

Shanker is a Hindu, and a worshipper of Vishnu, to the absolute exclusion of the other two members of the Hindu trinity. One afternoon in Benares he begged off from duty, without assigning a reason as usual. Later in the day, we encountered him coming up from his dip in the Ganges, which I suppose washed away his small offences committed against ourselves, in the matter of making off with loose change and petty pice. I have noticed that the boy is becoming gradually inoculated with civilized ideas after six weeks of contact with his American mistresses. One day last week his face fairly beamed with joy, and we made him produce the cause. He had been to the bazaar, and had invested in a pair of cinnamon-colored stockings, the first he ever owned in his life; and in order to make his vanity as little apparent to the other servants as possible, he had bought stockings of the exact shade of his bright brown skin. Shanker, having climbed forty rounds of his life's ladder barefoot, now proposes in future to proceed more comfortably. The rest of his clothes are also undergoing transformation: instead of the gorgeous butterfly in red and gold turban and brilliant sash in which we found him, he now insists on leaving off his cumberbund; so at the end he will probably reverse the natural butterfly method of doing things, and turn into a black-trousered and check-coated worm. You should hear his attempted English to appreciate it. Anything more funny I never imagined. His meaning can only be guessed at, and his face never changes expression in spite of the fits of laughing which overcome B. and myself at some of his speeches. Shanker wears a bang of oily black hair, and two very curly love-locks in front of each ear, always plastered down in place, over a full beard of the same silk-like texture. I never know when he eats his two daily meals, for he is always *en evidence.* Call out, "Shanker," and the echo answers, "Mem sahib?" a long musical tone on the end, which sounds like "Sabe."

Shanker's accomplishments are innumerable, and his occupations varied. He is our general manager, our treasurer; speaks the languages as interpreter; is courier and guide in one; makes our beds, and sleeps with one eye open at night on a rug outside our door; puts on a white starched linen garment above his bare feet, and waits on us at table; sits on the box when we drive; opens carriage doors; brings hot water; loads up our traps, camel-like, in travelling, — duties for which he feels munificently rewarded by twenty rupees a month, and an allowance of four annas a day for his food, which is *dol*, or curry and rice with tea. At the stations he secures our first-class carriage, stows away our boxes, and tips the guard that we may not be disturbed in our journey. This done, he rushes off with his worldly possessions in his carpet-bag, on which is tied a pewter tea-pot without a spout. With this he enters his third-class carriage, which is like the open street-cars in New York, and where the natives are crowded together so closely that they must sit upright and have no chance of resting or sleeping during the night.

We are stopping at Laurie's Hotel, — in the midst of a large compound of magnificent trees, once green, but at this season colored brown with dead leaves, dry and dusty. The house has only one floor, forming a crescent of columns; and our rooms

A BULLOCK CART AND SHANKER.

have an entrance from the dining-room, and also one from the garden compound, where only a bamboo screen separates us from the usual inhabitants of such premises, — the native coolies, who have here their huts with the chickens and the crows.

It is Sunday morning when we arrive; and in the afternoon we hunt up Miss S.,[1] — a niece of a former distinguished American statesman, — who has lived for twenty-three years in Allahabad. Our native syce insists that he knows just where to find her, and first lands us in the heart of the native quarter, at a little white Presbyterian church, queerly contrasting with the mud huts of the vicinity. On the street and in the bazaar, everything is going on as usual. The tailors cut and snip in open air, sitting cross-legged before their work, in full view of passers-by; every part of the article in hand is done before the purchaser's own eyes, every part is in the process of completion in the very place where the finished thing is sold. They are the native bazaars, all without windows; the interior is dark, floored with mud, with clay walls and ceiling, and barren of furniture. We step inside the church, and see a congregation of dark people, — the men on one side of the centre aisle, and the women on the other, in their white chuddahs, and thin white veils over their heads. The preacher

[1] Since writing the above, her friends have received news of her death from cholera in Allahabad.

was reading in Hindustani, but so impressively that I could almost understand his meaning from the expression he gave to his musical language. An old native handed me a Hindustani hymn-book, which I could not read; so we only remained a few moments, and were re-directed to "Miss Sahib," as she is known in Allahabad.

In a pretty compound, rose-garlanded and vine-twisted, stands the thatched-roof bungalow, where we find the little American lady. Here she has lived sixteen years, her only companion an English assistant, nurse and doctor all in one. We think she has a pretty plain time of it, poor little woman; her companion only cares to discuss two subjects. These begin the day and end the hours of after-dinner talk, accompany the drives and small excursions of the two little ladies; and, perhaps, their restless dreams conjure up two gaunt and hideous spectre incarnations of their day thought. These two subjects, the Alpha and Omega of their conversation, the grim supplanters of woman's small talk and gossip, are "theology" and the "dispensary." A dear old ayah, soft-footed and gentle, takes good care of her little mistress; and, besides, there are more servants to manage the house and to be managed. There is the sweeper, who can only attend to his department, and never enters the cuisine; for an Indian servant only performs the duties of his hereditary line of business, — and so on to *syces*,[1] *bhisties*,[2] and *dhobies*.[3] All these servants come to this considerate mistress with great willingness, and are as devoted as native gratitude permits.

We enjoyed Allahabad after this with our accomplished guide, to whom all the Urdu and Hindustani spoken is as her own language, and we never wearied her complaisance in asking a million questions about India and her friends, the Indians. In the native city, deep in its narrow lanes and curving streets, there is one building, which is on quite different lines from its neighbors. Here, every morning at an early hour, comes Miss S.'s dog-cart, with the syce holding the white cotton umbrella over his little mistress's determined and courageous head and gold-rimmed eye-glasses. It is the new dispensary, this plain, substantial building, — the result of Miss S.'s determined energy, and is her pride and joy. We also came there one morning in that little cart, and found the two assistants already busy and hard at work in the bare, cheerless interior, — no carpets, no pictures or hangings or chairs, where no occupants could be seen except the three little doctors. Outside the office door, on the enclosed piazza, and squatting on the hard cement floor of the room, were the patients, forming a circle of painful and expectant faces.

[1] *Syce*, an Indian coachman. [2] *Bhistie*, water-carrier.
[3] *Dhobie*, laundry-man.

They were ill, that was evident, but patient, like all the East; and each would wait her turn to be summoned to Miss S.'s side, registered in a book, numbered, and questioned as to the trouble, if treated before, etc. — and all without complaining, just simply stating their sickness, and answering questions. It was so unutterably sad. A few persons had companions to help them walk the distance to the infirmary; and high-caste women were carried here in *purdahs* by coolies, closely concealed from all view. Medicines are given, operations performed, and women cured, who otherwise would never have been well again. Their only hope, their comfort, and their very existence they owe to Miss S. No man would be permitted to see or touch them. The position of women here is so inferior to that of men, that a physician is rarely called should they be ill.

In a rich Hindu family, it sometimes happens that as a last resource a doctor is summoned. His patient is then closely concealed from view by *purdahs* (heavy curtains), which are parted only wide enough to thrust through the hand or show the tongue. From these unsatisfactory evidences alone, the doctor makes up his mind as to the treatment; and it sometimes happens that, owing to the distrust of medical assistance in the Hindu religion, a test of the doctor's knowledge is made by the husband, in having a well person instead of the sick one placed behind the purdah.

I would say a few words, by the way, on the subject of the dispensary. It is only useful, in the first place, to a few of the many sick and suffering native women in Allahabad. Hundreds of women are dying of utter neglect, — there not being sufficient funds available for the dispensary to pursue the work of healing in their homes, should the patients be too ill to return for treatment. So they are often lost track of after a few visits, and probably die in their homes, to the undeserved discredit of their physicians. We felt very indignant at the way in which Miss S.'s splendid medical knowledge was cramped and her wonderful energy curtailed, from her not being able to control the financial expenditures needed for her dispensary. A little more encouragement and aid would furnish the plain, bare rooms with beds and a few needed accessories, adding wards, in the hospital manner, where native women could be properly cared for and attended by competent nurses. The Lady Dufferin Hospitals would seem to supply this need of medical care for native women; but I have heard them spoken of in the East in a slighting manner, from the readiness to employ native nurses and doctors after only a few months' training and practice. It only requires a few months of this hospital life for any woman to gain a diploma, whether or no she has any natural gifts, qualifications, or, in fact, intelligence enough to acquire the art of healing. The medical missionaries speak very guardedly and with great reserve when talking of these institutions; but one can easily detect a *soupçon* of disapproval, when they say, "It is a step certainly, but not a great one, in the right direction."

At half past ten the last medicine had been given, and we all left for a walk. It was in such a narrow street that no horse harnessed to anything whatever could possibly come through it. We stopped before a one-story, white plaster house, pushing open a low wooden door without further ceremony. The doctor had been very often to this house professionally; this time she was bringing us to the residence of a Brahmin pundit, to see the women of a Hindu zenana, who never before had looked at a white lady except Miss S. We lift a thick-wadded curtain that separates the public from the private parts of the house, and enter a small courtyard planted with fruit-trees and shrubbery, around which are the women's apartments. Zenana means simply a "woman." Many of the Indians speak of their wives as their zenanas. The Hindu idea of a family is made to embrace not only the head of the house, but the sons, the grandsons, and the great-grandsons, as well as the brothers and their descendants. The Hindu boy bridegroom always takes his new wife to his father's house, where a room is given him; so the different members of these clannish families live together. The money brought in by the family is placed in one common fund, presided over by the lord of the manor. The zenana apartments are quite distinct from those occupied by the men; and during the day husband and wife never meet for conversation, and only see each other while they are being served at table by the women, who never think of touching food until the men have enjoyed their meals and gone out of the house to business or some place of amusement. It is a strict rule of the Hindu religion that all food must be cooked and prepared by the wives, who do everything about the house, unassisted except in the most menial labor. The inner rooms occupied by the zenana ladies have very small windows, too high to look into the street: the Vedas command that a woman must never stand at a door or look out of a window. From this prison life, she enters the world rarely; and when she goes, it is in a palanquin, carried on the shoulders of four men. When paying a visit to her father's house, which she is occasionally permitted to do, the palanquin is carried into the courtyard; when the woman enters, the doors slide back into their places, and over all is spread a purdah, so carefully veiled and guarded she can neither see nor be seen by any one.

The ladies of the Brahmin household were taken entirely unawares by our visit. We found them sitting on a charpoy, in a plain, undecorated room, in simple muslin saris, without their feast-day ornaments and jewels, — only the splendid gems which hung from the nose-rings proved they possessed anything in the line of luxury. The apartment was so lacking in comfort, or any suggestion of ease, that you were simply startled by the stern reality of the bare, uneventful, listless lives of the women, which you always had pictured in your own mind as living among the fanciful glories of the "Arabian Nights." We were told these glories, in the way of hangings, rugs, and draperies, are only brought out for marriages or other feasts, and that the usual appearance of the richest Indian household is similar to the one we are now visiting. A beautiful Cashmerian woman, with the rich olive complexion of a brunette and soft dreamy eyes, blackened under the lids with "the kohol's jetty dye, to give that long, dark language to the eye," and her little boy, in embroidered velvet jacket and tinsel cap, and nothing else besides for raiment, who shrank back in his mother's arms in terror at our strange faces and dress, made a beautiful Madonna picture in Oriental colors.

A NATIVE HINDU FAMILY.

Like everything else that is beautiful in the East, the finest women come from the Vale of Cashmere. This one was the favorite wife of the Brahmin; and it is unusual among this aristocratic sect to have more than one wife, except in extraordinary cases, and then the oldest woman becomes the ruler of the zenana, whom all the others are expected to respect and obey. Through our interpreter, we talked pleasantly with these ladies for an hour, and were charmed by their gentle and friendly manner, which left an impression of cordiality, sweetness, and dignity, which will linger long in our memories.

At length we must leave; and would say, "Good-by, we are going," when Miss S. warned us in time that this would be an unpardonable breach of Indian etiquette. When a visitor to a Hindu house leaves, the custom is not to say, "I am going." — that would very properly shock the hostess; but the leave-taking is like this: the guest salaams her hostess and says, "I come;" to which the lady sweetly replies, "Come again."

To-day we drove out to the Great Melah in a high barouche. Two postilions ran ahead and cleared the way, else our progress might have been fatally terminated at some sharp corner. The *melah* is a high feast, which takes place once every year at a point where the yellow Ganges flows into the blue Jumna River. What a sight! Thousands of pilgrims from all over India and the great Thibetian table-land come here to bathe in the Ganges, — old and lame, young and beautiful, rajahs and beggars, — camping in their bamboo huts on the plain by the riverside, among the mud-covered holy men; for bathing in the Ganges will destroy all sins, past, present, or future. We stopped to speak to a group of fakirs, sitting around some dead embers, their faces painted with colored clays, their hair so matted and covered with ashes, that it indeed seemed impossible to realize that these were the "wise men from the East."

The rôle of a fakir is assumed by Brahmins and many who are not Brahmins. It is a profession in India, — a profession of asceticism or sainthood. The regime required to become a Hindu saint is severe and terrible. They are first obliged to become students, learning from the older priests the sacred scriptures of the Vedas; they then "pass into the silent life of prayer," and spend years of meditation in the jungle, to complete their self-sacrifice; and, as a final test, remain seven years in the world. In India, I met a Swedish lady who told me that she spent an evening at a ball in Bombay in the society of a Hindu, who charmed her by his conversation, his wit, and brilliancy. Being thoroughly in sympathy with this lady's thought about the Eastern religion, he was moved to tell her when they parted that he — this courtly, charming man — was passing through the test which succeeds the mud of the fakir's life, in order to attain his sainthood.

Allahabad is a beautiful, regular town, built on the banks of the Jumna River. The European bungalows are low, one-storied buildings, surrounded by gardens tastefully laid out, with vines falling like a curtain in a shower of purple blossoms from over the *porte cochère.* The garrison occupies Akbar's old fort on the banks of the river. In the olden time the fort was the site of a much venerated Hindu shrine. It was considered a sacred place on account of a tree which grows without sun or light in the midst of the dark subterranean chapel. The English have never quite dared to close the shrine to the native Hindus, who still believe the tree thrives as it did in ancient times. The English officer who showed us about the fort, and with whom we visited the place, told us under his breath that the Brahmins, who have imposed this fiction for many hundreds of years on the people, continue to do so under the British government; and twice, the officer said, the dead tree had been cut down and taken away in the night by the priests, and he had himself aided in replacing it by a new one.

CHAPTER VIII.

CALCUTTA.

January 23.

A BREEZE is blowing, and it is from the Bay of Bengal. There is a breath-touch of cold at nightfall, and it comes from the Himalayas. From all the open windows and balconies a gentle air reminds you of flowers, and it is the scent of the lotus; and leaves come flying in the wind, and they are from the gardens of the Viceroy of India's palace. From my window-seat you can look off, and ships are lying close to the docks, their tall masts traced against the Indian sky, and they are anchored on the Ganges; so that you know this is Calcutta and we are in the presidency of Bengal,—the heart of the great and splendid India.

You must say "India" almost reverently, not lightly, because it means so much; it is so wonderful; and we are, or seem to be, present at its death, or the passing away of its latest conquerors, the Moguls. In Italy and other lands ruins are reminders of past days, so long gone by that you talk of them as mere phantoms, and scarcely believe them as realities; but here the great palaces and wonderful mosques have to do with people who, as it were, have just left, and are not yet forgotten. The palaces are perfect, or nearly so, — abandoned so recently by the emperors, and only yesterday transformed into forts and high courts of justice.

I am beginning to take in the vast empire we call India, and my imagination is playing riot to-day in fancies. What wonderful people these Bengalis are! There are fifteen thousand learned university graduates in Calcutta alone, — among them high-caste Brahmin students, who have first studied and learned English, and then their own language, besides Sanscrit, which is the language of their books, the literary language of India.

At six o'clock yesterday morning I opened my eyes and saw Calcutta from the railway carriage, where we spent a very good night, wrapped in rugs and with innumerable cushions. No one else occupied the carriage; each had a wide sliding bed to sleep on, and there were thirteen different packages in our compartment for comfort. Two young Englishmen next door outnumbered us, however, as I counted thirty boxes and traps come out of their carriage this morning. No one minds luggage in this country. Twenty coolies were the very least that we required to land our luggage, and we could easily have had two hundred by a nod to them.

They walked from the train across the station platform, carrying our heavy boxes on their heads, and waited at the carriage door to receive their two pice each, — about one and a half cents, which satisfied their modest aspirations. A cart made of long reeds of bamboo laid between two wheels and drawn by bullocks, took our heavy boxes, while we mounted a palki-gharri, and drove to the Great Eastern Hotel. The palki proper is a square black box, — the gondola of Calcutta, — always black and brightly varnished, carried by coolies, one at each end of the two long poles on which it rests. You enter a sliding door, and recline on your back when being carried about.

The Great Eastern is the best inn that the capital affords, but greatly behind the times in every modern invention. Its situation is good, facing the Government House, on the opposite side of the park; and there are plenty of green trees and flowers in sight from the wide verandas. The hotel is full to overflowing, as it usually is in January, — the season in Calcutta. A servant shows us rooms in an annex in a side street, which they call a terrace, but it looks like a shed, roughly built, with unpolished board partitions, and furnished with three beds, varying in size, but composed alike of iron slats, mercifully hidden from sight by a thin mattress spread over them. They promise better things, however, later on.

We had really determined to take a good rest, but the temptation to go and see something was so strong that in the afternoon we set off for a Hindu native bazaar. Our gharri is a most disreputable equipage for the capital of all the Indies; but the coachman has a sort of white and purple turban, like a life-preserver, on his head, and a white gown like a chorister's over his brown legs, and two other men stand up behind, while our boy "Shanker" sits on the box, with his arms folded, and his bare feet braced on the dashboard in perfect line with the coachman, which should add dignity enough to make us contented, in spite of the fact that the horses' dinner of hay is trailing down from a loose bundle on the front seat, and a pack of the same is tied up in muslin wrappings under the carriage. After a long drive, we reached an open street, lined with native houses of a rather good class, stopped at a certain number in Upper Circular Road, and entered the grounds of Lily Cottage, where the great Hindu reformer, Keshub Chunder Sen, lived for many years.

It was ladies' day at the festival, and a thick-wadded curtain fenced securely all masculine glances from the bazaar. Among the dense old peepul-trees (worshipped, no doubt, by the forefathers of these very Hindu ladies who are selling French dolls and European toys) were the high-caste women of Calcutta, — the representatives of the families of the

Brahmo-Somaj, founded by Sen, nearly all of whom have discarded caste and superstition, and are the Liberals of India. No one spoke English; and among so many women, no others but ourselves wore European dress, — all were draped alike in saris, bordered with gold, and wore nose-rings, and ear-rings extending from the top to the lobe of the ear.

Through the vista made by branching trees we wandered aimlessly towards a white, pillared, Corinthian house. A magnificent, broad-shouldered young Indian, looking like a Roman senator in his white toga, came down from his house along the great flight of steps leading to the ground-floor. It was Sen's son; he spoke to us in perfect English, and explained with pride, that, although the Liberals were every day shaking off the seclusion which guards their women, he would not yet be allowed to enter the bazaar on ladies' day for fear of offending some of the Conservatives. Then he pointed to his father's grave in a square garden-enclosure adjoining the house; it was a white shaft, simply inscribed with a Bible verse and his name. The daughter of Sen is married to the rajah of Cooch Bahar, one of the richest and most European of native princes. The maharanee, dressed in a white brocaded sari, with a *rivière* of diamonds and pearls, — a very large, handsome woman, very self-possessed, — was in charge of a stall, and sold her wares with all the coquetry and attraction of an English woman. We were told that Sen was more of a Unitarian than anything else, and that the Brahmos gave the missionaries more trouble than orthodox Hindus; also, that many of his so-called "reforms" were in reality only in name; and though he discountenanced child-marriage, Keshub Chunder Sen could not resist the temptation of marrying his daughter as a child to the rich rajah. The Brahmo-Somaj has suffered since Sen's death from a division in the ranks. Mosemdhal, the right-hand man of his master, wished to occupy his vacant place; but Sen's son objected to any person taking his father's pulpit, saying, "My father once present there, is always present." Keshub Chunder Sen was educated in England, where he is said to have once preached from a text taken from seven different religions.

The social question now most discussed everywhere in India is "Hindu Child-Marriage" and the "Age-of-Consent Bill." It seems to be the impression that a rebellion must come one day to India, and that it will be caused by the English lack of decision and firmness in dealing with the question of "child-marriage," which is so clearly wrong to the best interests of India. The reports published are exaggerated, and do not really represent the opinions of the native women in the zenanas, who are most anxiously awaiting some relief. In olden times, before Mahometan rule began in Northern India, the women had greater freedom than those of civilized nations in the choice of a husband. Now, the Mahometan custom of early marriages is engrafted in that most susceptible of religions, Hinduism, and exaggerated into making a child a bride.

Calcutta is not pretty, or even picturesque, — a long, flat city, not much more than a mile wide, stretching for a space of seven miles along the banks of the river Hugli, a slow and muddy branch of the greater Ganges. There is only one good street, — wide, well-paved, and shady. This is in the European quarter; and here are to be found the fine houses that have given to Calcutta the name of the City of Palaces. The Doric columns, broad verandas, and windows with balconies surrounding them, make the place attractive. And then there is the *maidan*, — a plain about a mile and a quarter long, between the river and the fort, — where the races take place; and the Eden Gardens, the Rotten Row of Calcutta, where the driving rolls along in the afternoon. The native streets are narrow, dirty, and crowded. They are lined with native shops; and the first thing that attracts your attention is the way in which everything a man has to sell is in full view of the passer-by. There are no windows, in which the best specimens are arranged as attractively as possible; but the shopkeeper sits, or stands, behind his goods, always smoking his hookah. The shops are open early in the morning, and are closed about eleven o'clock, at which time the merchant leaves for his bath and breakfast. In the afternoon about two o'clock they re-open, and remain so until nine or ten in the evening. Bengalis and other natives are the only customers; and so small are many of the transactions of the shopkeepers that shells are used as money. The houses of the poor people are built of mud or matting, with thatched roofs. They have no windows, only little grated openings to admit air and light; and here caste obliges them to live as they have always lived. The shoemakers form a quarter, the jewellers another, and the brass-workers, like their fathers before them, hammer and tinker in the brass bazaar. The Bengalis are very clever, and crowd the government colleges, so anxious are they to pass the examination and become eligible for government service. Calcutta is certainly the Oxford of India,— a great university centre. The Bengalis learn English very readily, and their study of the language is far more profound and earnest than that of college boys in England. And a native who knows English will generally wish his wives to be educated, which accounts for the success of zenana work in India.

January 25.

From a balcony, in clear warm sunshine, under an Eastern sky, with the noble figures of Arabians, Persians, and Indians, in brilliant cashmeres, thronging the streets, we witnessed the *entrée* into Calcutta of the czarowitch. All day the excitement was intense, for the Indian people dearly love a "tomasha," and were formerly ruled by pageants. Only in the East can one witness such a glorious spectacle. Just beyond us is Government House, a great, yellow stucco Versailles, surrounded by parks and fountains; while from the high gateways, topped by the British lions, stretches a gold and red line of the queen's soldiers along the esplanade to the station, where twenty-one guns are sounded as the czarowitch touches the Indian soil. And soon, down Calcutta's broad streets, between the guard's presented arms, came the mounted body-guard of the viceroy, the crack corps of India, — splendid natives in red uniforms, and gold twisted turbans covering their dark heads. Most effective in the procession were long slender flag-poles with tiny red and white flags, each lancer holding one with the right hand, and managing a fractious Arabian horse with the other. Then the heroes of Indian wars rode by, flashing with silver and red decorations.

And now comes a pause in the procession; then all the people wave and cheer frantically. Six horses appear, ridden by flag-lancers, drawing the state carriage, in which is seated Lord Lansdowne in uniform, and beside him, the blond, young czarowitch. He wears his silver Russian helmet, on the front of which is a white and silver aigrette twelve inches high, a blue and silver-embroidered uniform, and a braided white-cloth jacket edged with sable thrown over one shoulder. His expression is unaffected and dignified. More state carriages and magnificent trappings are coming; and Prince George of Greece and two other princes ride by, each having outriders and postilions, followed by the artillery, making a clanking, war-like sound in passing. Close in the rear follows a man, the most concerned of them all, the anxious and worried chief of police, on whom rests the tremendous responsibility for the safety in India of the poor hunted czarowitch. (I give you a choice of spelling; the prince's luggage is labelled, "Le Casarewitch.") Woe unto England, if any nihilistic attempt should succeed here!

"So passed they through the gates" of Government House. And soon after appeared a cortége of Indian princes, — the rajahs of ancient line, whose coaches have a *passée* look about the linings and painted panels. But the princes themselves! — the descendants of padishahs, the nawabs of Bengal, the guicowars, and the peshwas, whose draperies, overloaded with jewels and heavy embroideries, outrival even the priestly vestments of

Catholic countries. And up and down Calcutta streets stretches a long vista of color, — Cashmerian colors, in purple and red effects, "like a vast bed of tulips," — for the order had been given that all the town should keep high festival. A scene of Eastern splendor past all imagination. No doubt, all this time the imperial visitor is vainly longing for his tub, and a cup of Russian tea; but we are taking ours, and must rest for the ball to-night.

January 26.

"The Aide-de-camp of the Viceroy of India commands your presence, Monday evening, January 26, to meet His Imperial Highness, the Czarowitch."

The clock was striking ten as we followed Shanker and his best red turban down the steps of the Great Eastern to our barouche, where we found two dingy Eastern servants salaaming before the open carriage door. When we are seated inside, they mount behind, and look as dignified and important as postilions could possibly appear, with bare black legs wrapped to the knees in dusky muslin, green coats, and huge white muslin turbans. Shanker springs on to the box, and we fall in line with a stream of Calcutta's private carriages, advancing slowly along the softly lighted quarter of a mile, which stretches from the viceroy's park gates.

Red-coated servants, with yellow and red rope-twisted turbans and gold waistbands, show the way to the anteroom, where we leave coats and wraps. Flowers and palms line the wide corridors, and more red-coated servants flank the entrance to the reception-room, where we find Lady Lansdowne, with the czarowitch and foreign princes at her side. She is tall, very slender, and high-bred; wears a long silvery gray gown, with ropes of handsome pearls about her neck. The czarowitch seems the very perfection of unaffected simplicity and good-natured manners, — blond, blue-eyed, and boyish.

The ballroom blazes with light and color. The polished floor throws back the reflection of the brilliant lights, and makes constellations of star-like jets between the polished marble columns which lined the ballroom. The room is filled with a moving throng of glittering nationalities. The glimmer of gorgeous raiment and the flashes of jewels of fabulous value look like a dream of the "Arabian Nights." Native princes, maharajahs, and chieftains sparkle and glitter with gems and embroideries. Here is Cooch Bahar, a rajah of rajahs in Bengal. He wears a most wonderful diamond tiara, fastened just above his forehead in a white-silk turban, coiled about his head until hair, forehead, ears, all, are completely covered; and a collar of large diamonds falls from his throat in gleaming strands until it reaches his shoulders. An embroidered white cashmere coat extended to his knees. The maharanee, daughter of Chunder Sen, is here, in a strange mixture of barbaric and civilized dress. She is the only emancipated rajah's wife in India. Her husband, educated at Cambridge, insisted on making a love-match at eighteen with a girl whose father was once a clerk in a Bengal bank, although the founder of the Brahmo-Somaj. A fascinating, dark-skinned prince, who belongs to an historical family of Mysore, is presented to us, — Shahzada Mahomet Furrokshah, grandson of Tippoo, the prince who made the English under Wellesley suffer defeat in the Deccan. Just shut your eyes, and in fancy you hear the most cultivated English voice speaking to you. Open them, and before you is a tall, dark man, with glistening teeth, lustrous eyes, and exquisite manners, showing his barbarian ancestry in the high black velvet cap, with a broad rim of diamonds and emeralds entirely encircling it. A blazing star just in front holds a white aigrette, tipped with diamonds and rubies. But, above all, look at the ruby which is hanging just over his brows; and fancy the diamond chain and collar which keep the neck quite as stiff as a pillory, and look as uncomfortable. Think of the gold-belted, gem-studded robe, and hear this diamond prince speaking the most polished English and paying graceful compliments in the most civilized way; imagine many rajahs, haughty, silent, and solemn, even more bejewelled, with studded swords attached by diamond chains, resembling gayly-dressed puppets in a masquerade, — and you can fancy now what the wealth of the Indies really means.

The transition state from barbaric clothes to civilized dress in the East is certainly amusing. One rajah reminds us of a dull moth-worm just emerging to the butterfly state. The high, three-storied, diamond crown of his ancestors is perched in Oriental manner above his long silky black hair. He still wears the native robe of white embroidered cashmere, fitting tight to the waist and full to the knee, where it meets a pair of black-and-white checked trousers, and patent leather ties fresh from Regent Street. An Oriental priest of the Greek church towers above them all, by reason of the small smoke-stack on his head, draped in purple like his plain trailing robes. A massive gold chain hangs to his waist, with a blazing Greek cross. The Burmese are as quaint and unlike other people as possible. The little Burmese princesses are short, very brown, and look very unhappily out of their beady black eyes at this new element of European life in which they move. The flash of uniforms, the dazzling red-and-gold coats of officers of European and native regiments, the jewels of the Europeans, clash, sparkle, scintillate in dazzling visions. Alone, unequalled in magnificence, a ball at the viceroy's is the meeting of centuries of Oriental despotism with the representatives of the world's highest civilization; and it seems to me the link between the past and the present is the young czarowitch, — a Cæsar, and at the same time a father of his people.

January 28.

A delicious impression remains of a lovely afternoon, — a drive through lawns so close and green and carpet-like that one would fancy it was England; an England where palms and pomisetta shrubbery are flourishing out of doors in January. It was the afternoon of the garden-party at Government House, — a "tomasha" of such importance that all Calcutta had worn an expectant look for days. We stopped in front of a large carpeted tent, where the red-coated band played, and where groups of girls in pretty muslins and men in every style of Oriental and civilized garb walked together over the paths and through the flowering trees of that rich tropical garden. In the centre of it was the vice-regal party, — Lord and Lady Lansdowne, the Highland aides-de-camp, and the Russian czarowitch, dressed like an English gentleman. The glamour gone, one begins to criticise: his neck is large; he has a pallid complexion; you discover he is a small man without that heavy uniform and fur-edged cape. What a surprise! However, the trace of sweetness and gentleness is still there, and his lips curl with a certain hauteur; and, above all, he is self-possessed and brave, — unconsciously so. From a tent, tea and cakes are served in profusion, with wines and ices. Standing near us is Sen, transformed from the white draped figure of yesterday, in a classic Bengali dress, to a European cockney, cast in bronze.

January 29.

Morning, early morning, with a fresh and lovely breeze, and worth the effort made to get out of bed to enjoy it. B. and I walked forty minutes in and around the Eden Gardens of Government House, meeting galloping steeds, ridden by the fortunates, whom I could hardly resist asking to dismount, that I might once more tear around on a dear horse. This afternoon was race-day, and we went to the meeting of the Calcutta Turf Club, — the races where the rich nabobs of Bengal appeared most unsportsmanlike in gorgeous velvet and satin robes, heavy with embroideries, with cashmere shawls thrown scarf-like over their shoulders. I cannot say much for the appointments, stand, etc.; but the course was good, and the horses ran well. W. M. Beresford's colors — light blue and black cap — were popular, but unfortunate. The horses and ponies were from Australia; hardly any others could endure the climate.

At five o'clock every evening all Calcutta goes

forth in fine array to hear the military band play in the Eden Gardens; and it befell us also to spend one hour there among the blossoms and over-spreading trees. And when the sun first tinges all Nature with its mellow tinted light, and then hastens away behind the western hills, and men's shadows lengthen as the days decrease; and when the music pauses, and you hear in the hedges "the lemon petals gently fall within the windless Indian night," and all the moving throng is strangely lulled to quiet by the spell made by the moonbeams, and saddened as if some wistful, unknown dream had shaped itself in thought, — suddenly at our side bends a dark-eyed Indian prince in salutation, who is, though dowered by birth with proud descent,

> "In speech
> Right gentle, yet so wise; princely of mien,
> Yet softly-mannered; modest, deferent,
> And tender-hearted, though of fearless blood."

Taking inspiration from the scene, he speaks to us of Nature and the glories of the Himalayas, and beauty; and ending, wishes for us good fortune and a safe journey, and says, "Salaam."

"Salaam," — how much this word expresses! what a word, a language in itself! in how many forms it comes to all, — sometimes, oftentimes, bringing gladness, and again finishing, forever, some international romance begun on shipboard, and in the tropics of Ceylon, lingering on in India, dying slowly, and ending with the message, "Salaam!" "Salaam" begins the day; you open your eyes, and the ayah parts the purdahs, bends her black and dusky head over the pillow, and smiles, whispering, "Good-morning, salaam." Your "boy" comes in now with chota-hazri, and balancing the tray recklessly with one hand, bows low over the tea and toast, with his right hand moving slowly from his eyes down to the waist, and repeats, "Salaam." After hot water and a sponge have encouraged you for a day of rounds of excitement, you leave your room; and white-turbaned dark figures rise from hidden corners up and down the hall, noiseless as magic, and bow down profoundly as you pass — "Salaam." You are now going for a drive; and from the hotel entrance ten coolies start off to volunteer to scare up a palki, and before going, stumble over one another in one profound "salaam." The blind beggar, whom you have almost run down in your *gharri*,[1] or who sits on his ragged mat by the roadside, is imploring your charity in a beseeching wail. "Salaam" — "alms," he moans, — "give, good people, or I die!" You toss a pice to a little quaint black figure, whose anatomy is all visible, with no vestige of a rag for clothing, and who has earned your admiration

[1] Carriage.

for his wonderful running of miles of the way, keeping up to the horses, and beating his little chest to indicate hunger, crying between breaths, "Salaam, salaam!" You have sent a note by a coolie messenger; it was received, you know that. The answer came, "My compliments, — salaam. We have it in the shops. Shall I send it home for you, Miss Sahib? Very well, salaam." We are driving up to a beautiful bungalow. The syce jumps down, and takes your card, moving his open fingers before his face on receiving it, — "salaam." On the wide veranda stand our friends. The servants make a general "salaam" in concert as if to slow music, when you enter the door and pass into the house. The suave, polished descendant of Mahomet receives you in the anteroom; and, before taking your offered hand, bends his head most respectfully, and graciously says in greeting, his ancient, time-honored Mahometan "salaam." A beautiful woman is sitting on Persian carpets, in the midst of Oriental hangings and draperies; she rises, looks down, veils her beautiful face with one jewelled hand, which she sweeps with a graceful gesture from her brows downward. She is saying your welcome to her house, that you may enjoy all she enjoys, and be happy; and what she almost murmurs in softest voice is, "salaam." The gracious lady's soft-footed Hindu women move gently about in white draperies, and hand you tea from lovely Eastern cups; they approach you almost timidly with "salaam." In the doorway, in silk and fine muslin, stands the ayah, in whose strong arms, tinkling with silver bangles and armlets, is the beautiful boy, the very flesh-and-blood idol of all the house of Seyd. His big eyes are sparkling and black with excitement; his short black hair is smooth under a silver-embroidered tight cap. From his head to his feet, the royal little fellow is wrapped in a long, purple satin coat, heavy with gold embroidery, and brightly lined with gorgeous gold satin. We, the first Europeans his dear little eyes have ever seen, must be properly saluted; and baby's wee little fingers, dimpled hands, and wonderful rings close over the grave, small face, and in childish language he lisps, "Talaam, Mem Tahib." One really wonders if a Vedic angel will stand on the summit of Mount Meru, and dismiss the wretched, and welcome the blest into the heaven of Indra, with a well-worn "salaam." "Salaam, good-by," — I shall soon say this with sorrow to India, this wonderful India, brilliant, incomparable, romantic, but sad, — so sad, a land of regrets to many hopeful ones with lives wrecked in the service of the English Empress and her unappreciative government.

CHAPTER IX.

BENARES AND THE BRAHMINS.

January 31.

IT is Saturday morning, bright, clear, and cloudless, as only this Indian climate can be on occasions. Thursday evening, at half-past nine, we were just leaving Calcutta, driving down through the maidan, over the broad road across the Hugli Bridge, and into a roomy railway-carriage reserved for us at the station, where a mattress was spread out by Shanker, who had been there two hours before, attending to the baggage, — faithful dog that he is. We soon went to sleep, and, like the good little girl in the song, "knew no more until the break of day."

At six o'clock the next morning we found we had slept through the great Bengal Presidency, and were opening our eyes on Oude, the ancient kingdom where so many great Indian kings have lived and fought their battles. With laudable foresight, Shanker appears with a brass tray and smoking chai, and we also produce some good bread and jam from the lunch-basket; and at ten o'clock we met Miss S—— at Mogul Serai, the junction for Allahabad and Benares. Now every moment is one of intense excitement, until we at last cross the sacred river on the wide arches which span it, over which moves a constant procession of pilgrims, each one carrying in one hand a brass water-jug and a rope-basket of cotton meshes containing some rice and a blanket, slung on the two ends of a bamboo pole balanced from the shoulder, and in the other hand a staff, the badge of pilgrimage; all types, all grades, limping beggars and haughty rajahs, all with one thought, one aim, one ambition, — to reach Benares, the Hindu Rome, the most sacred city in their world.

The scene never changes. The multitudes surge on forever like great waves, now and then receding, only to gain new forces from the ocean of humanity, which is rolling on while we sleep and when we wake, through cold and hardship undaunted; for the journey is a path to heaven.

Far away, over the level plains of India, you see the moving line of pilgrims marching along the dusty high-roads, and filing through the foot-paths which bound the rice-fields. From the ice-hills of Thibet they come to breathe the parching air of Central India, — almost martyrs to the faith. From tropical Ceylon they come, suffering horribly from the night cold, having only one garment of about two yards of muslin for protection. Other poor creatures are provided with quilted comforters, made from gay cottons, which they wrap about the head and body; but their legs and feet are bare as in the hottest summer time. In the city streets trains are blocked and sometimes delayed for hours by the rush of pilgrims, and many thousands encamp about the open squares at night. Your first thought is that all the country is on the move; but you finally understand the meaning of it all, when in some holy place like Benares you observe the absolute bliss on the faces of those poor wretches who have at last, by years of hoarding and saving, cruel suffering from hunger and destitution during the journey, entered the place which to them is the "very gate of heaven."

After a drive of half an hour through the cantonment, we pass under a pretty archway, festooned with vines, and arrive in front of Clark's Hotel, situated in the centre of quiet gardens, like a little summer-house in the country. After tiffin we are beset by a native guide in yellow-striped calico trousers and red-striped coat of the same material, who, having picked up some English words, salaams us when we appear at the open door, and humbly beseeches to be allowed to accompany the party, saying, "What is one rupee, two rupees, to your respectable Highness?" which decides us, and we engage his services on the spot. The respect Hindus have for Europeans is delightful. We are always addressed as "your ladyship," except sometimes, when it is "Mem sahib," or "Miss sahib," which means "young lady;" and I am growing so accustomed to this side of the world that I shall not know how to conduct myself on its other side. In this well satisfied state of mind, the obsequious guide waiting, we discuss the question, What shall we see to-day? and three excited voices cry out at once with one accord, "The Ganges." Nothing makes you so easily realize that you are in the Antipodes as this mysterious word, especially if you happen to be a girl; and you recall terrible nursery tales of heathen mothers feeding their girl-babies to monster crocodiles, which you fancy still lie on the banks "with open, smiling jaws."

This river-worship of the Hindus is beautifully described in the oldest epic poem of India,[1] reciting the conquests of the mighty god Rama, and containing pictures in poetic language, — "the descent of the laughing and tremulous Ganga, the peerless daughter of Mena, the child of the old Himalaya." It relates that once upon a time, the valiant King Sagara wished to make a sacrifice: —

"But, lo! when all was prepared, when the sacred

[1] The Iliad of the East, — a selection of legends drawn from Valmiki's Sanscrit poem the Rāmāyana, by Frederika Richardson.

wood was piled, and the torch that yearned to consume it flamed in the hands of a priest, a serpent, under the form of Ananta, rose from the midst of the ground, and seizing the sacred horse, the victim promised to Brahma, disappeared with it, — swallowed up by the yawning earth. Surprise fell on the monarch Sagara; as for the Rishis and Brahmins and saintly anchorites, they were filled with hot indignation.

"Then the brow of the monarch grew red as the bolts of the flaming Indra. 'What would you have me do?' asked this furious tiger of men. 'There are sixty thousand heroes who call Sagara "father." Summon my sons forthwith,' shouted this enraged ruler of men.

"Then these sixty thousand princes came in haste, and found their magnanimous parent lying with his face in the dust, howling and biting the dust like an elephant struck by the hunter. They joined hands around him, and reverently performed a pradakshina. Then they asked what had shaken the balance of his equable humor.

"'Slay me this ravisher of the horse,' moaned forth the prostrate monarch. 'We will,' replied in one breath the sixty thousand heroes. At that the relieved Sagara rolled no more in the dust.

"The sixty thousand sons of Sagara explored the land far and wide; with lances, pickaxes, and clubs they threw up the earth and examined it; but nowhere could these indefatigable heroes discover a trace of their enemy.

"But broken by axes and spades, hewed and hacked and wofully injured, her innocent bosom gashed and mangled, the harmless goddess Prithivi mutely appealed to Heaven. A dolorous cry mounted up from serpents and lizards and beetles and myriads of living creatures whom the furious zeal of the heroes had wounded and maimed. 'Eternal Brahm,' they sobbed, 'deign to help us. Thou hast given us being; it is thine essence which quickens our blood.'

"Then the Eternal Fount of Existence answered them, gravely smiling: 'Out of evil comes good. These Sagarides who destroy life shall have their own lives taken from them; but from this act of theirs shall follow a blessing, — the bountiful, fecund, young Ganga shall bring her fresh bubbling waters to rejoice the hearts of all creatures.'

"The illustrious ruler of men, the anxious monarch Sagara, called to him the youthful Ansumat, whose limbs were like young fir-trees. 'Thy uncles are long in coming,' he said to the youthful warrior; 'my son, go in search of thy uncles, and bid them return here swiftly. My heart misgives me, Ansumat; bid them return very swiftly.'

"And so the valiant young warrior went forth to

seek for his uncles. The lordly Virupaksha, the magnanimous Mahapadma, the robust Saumanas, the sublime Himapandura, all greeted the nephew of sixty thousand uncles, and gave him news of his relatives. But when the indefatigable youth reached the infernal regions and beheld the state of his uncles, he fell on his face on the ground, uttering the most dolorous shrieks.

"Having bemoaned with tears and loud wailings the fate of these illustrious Sagarides, Ansumat looked round him anxiously for water with which to lave the cinders of these unfortunate heroes; for unless cleansed by lustrous waters, the dead are not admitted into paradise, the defilement of earthly passions rendering them unfit for the celestial abode. Looking round, Ansumat perceived, perched on the topmost bough of an acacia-tree, Garuda, the king of all the birds. 'Do not afflict yourself, most illustrious of men,' said this magnanimous bird. 'Thy sons cannot enter paradise till purified by the ceremony of lustrous waters; but this shall not take place until the Ganga shall quit the celestial regions and bring her sparkling wavelets to rejoice the inhabitants of the world.'

"For the space of one thousand years the afflicted monarch Sagara strove vainly to find some means of inducing the beautiful Ganga to abandon the house of the gods. At length Bhagiratha, the magnanimous son of Dilipa, abandoning his throne and the city, embraced the career of an anchorite on the wild slopes of the old Himalaya. Clad in a garment of skins, his head bared to the humors of heaven, keeping his passions in check, subsisting only on roots, alike tortured by heat and by cold, did the saintly anchorite importune the aid of the gods by the spectacle of his self-imposed sufferings.

"At the close of one thousand years, Brahma, the merciful guardian of men, appeared to him. 'Cease these inhuman macerations,' said the god. 'What is your request, Bhagiratha?' 'That these sixty thousand heroes might at length enter upon their bliss,' replied this worthy ancestor of Rama; 'that the Ganga might bring her purifying waters here below.' 'Your request is a hard one,' answered Brahma; 'for if the Ganga were to fall on the earth, her turbulent waters would overwhelm the world.'

"For another hundred years the saintly Bhagiratha continued his self-macerations. At the close of that time, Mahadeva appeared to the king of ascetics, and said, 'I am content, O most virtuous of men. I will sustain this river of purifying waters. I will, too, induce this bride of the immortals to quit her celestial home.'

"Then the glorious and generous immortal climbed the brow of the old Himalaya, and called to the fanciful Ganga, the queen amongst beautiful rivers: 'O child of the old Himalaya, whom the arms of Prithivi once cradled! this breast where then thou didst slumber is parched with a feverish thirst; therefore descend. O Ganga, Bride of the heavens! thy home is full of delight; the air is heavy with perfumes; the mirthful apsaras flit joyously hither and thither; the strains of the dreamy gandharvas thrill every year with rapture. The light here is golden, yet soft; the shade here is languid, yet warm; and the gods who dwell here are happy.'

"Then the large heart of the Ganga started and throbbed in her bosom; and without pause or reflection, the generous queen of all rivers rushed from the home of the gods in a burst of impetuous passion, singing, 'I come, O beloved! doubly beloved for thy sorrow.' Stepping forward, the generous Siva, in whose sight life is precious, received the great rush of waters, and upheld on his forehead the impulsive daughter of Mena, that in her generous fervor she might not overwhelm the earth. The gods, the Rishis and Brahmins, the Asuras, the Siddhas and Nagas, and all the hosts of earth and of heaven, came to witness this marvellous sight,—the joyous descent of the Ganga."

For a mile we drive through the native bazaars. Here may be found busy people working at various trades. It is marvellous how much the natives can manage to do with their feet and toes. Here, in the tailor quarter, are the dhurzies sewing industriously long breadths of beautiful silk, one end of which they hold with their toes. A native cook is also said to be very expert in this direction, and can make curry extremely well, using feet instead of hands. We leave the carriage at the river, and follow a flight of eighty steps, leading to the wonderful Ghauts.

One first sees Benares from the river, and no better view of it is possible to be obtained. The city is built on a crescent turn of the Ganges, on cliffs eighty or ninety feet high; and the astonishing effect produced by miles of stone steps descending from the heights above, crowned with palaces, temples, and mosques, — some in good preservation, others stained, broken, and fallen into the river,—is not like anything else in the world. Rich rajahs have built palaces here, which they occupy periodically, as other people have country-homes in different places; but the chief purpose of their annual visit to Benares is to wash away sins contracted in less holy places. The muddy and dirty Ganges seems to bear witness to the blackness of the aforesaid sins. A stream of flowers is constantly floating down the current of the river,—offerings made by the Hindus to the Goddess of the Water.

At the bathing Ghaut there were hundreds of pilgrims performing the most sacred act of their religion. Watching one man very particularly, we could see him wriggle and twist in the water, point his hands together, and bend his head very solemnly; take the water into the mouth, eject it; place some in the hollow of the hand, and offer it to the sun, the north, south, east, and west; clap it on the forehead, pat his head very devoutly, and genuflect like an Italian in Naples; then wash in the river his two pieces of linen, the one for the head and the other for the body; and afterwards perform the most meritorious act of all,—drink the water, and carry it away in lotas, perhaps many hundreds of miles, to be used for his devotions until the next pilgrimage. We see men here who have been twelve years doing the holy shrines of India, now wretched beggars, most miserable and poor, but fanatically happy.

I bought for half a rupee, from a pilgrim who had just left the river, a worn brass jar which he had just filled with the Ganges water. Perhaps this same lota has travelled many miles of Indian highways. Well, now that I have it, it must be put to a baser use,—in adorning an American home.

Farther on, boats were rowing slowly out in the stream, with groups of devotional Hindus carrying jars of brass, which they fill with flowers, and pour out in offerings to the river. On all sides were brightly painted floats, with wedding parties on board,—bright, jewelled women and their bridegrooms and friends, all wearing flower necklaces about their throats; and there were other holy men washing; and more women with bright brass jars praying beside the sacred waters,—the whole scene lighted up by an Eastern sun, bringing out the dazzling colors of the dress of the people, and the gilded domes of mosques and temples tipped in curious ornaments. This wealth of architectural glories on the river-front is amazing, unsurpassed; making one continually call out in exclamations of wonder and surprise.

Finally we sail past the pilgrims a mile or more toward the burning Ghaut. High on the bank are groups of women wailing and lamenting, "Call on Rama, brothers! Rama, O Rama, Rama! hear;" and in a hollow ravine below are three bodies prepared for burning. One is close to the water's edge, piled high with fagots; and five times around the pyre is going a man, the nearest male relative to the dead one. His head is shaven closely, except for one long lock; and with a brand of burning straw he lights the wood heaped up about the corpse, and "sets the red flame to the corners four, which crept and licked and flickered, finding out his flesh and feeding on it with swift, hissing tongues." Another pyre is smouldering, stirred up occasionally by the priests; and, horror of horrors! pariah dogs close by, who complete the unfinished destruction of the body by fire. Our guide said it was very costly to burn,—seven rupees, eight annas; but our companion said she burned her servants for one rupee. Only children and the very poor are thrown into the river; and sometimes when rowing one comes up to a dead body with half a dozen crows perched on it. One often sees people taken down to the side of the sacred stream to die, gaining thereby a direct entrance to the Hindu paradise.

Now we row slowly back, and the riverside is still lined with the pilgrims praying; and our guides point to one, calling him a "holy beggar." And why "holy beggar"? "Because he does not beg his bread, but gets it by subscription," is the unexpected answer.

Returning, we take a turn through the brass bazaar,—narrow streets with only one width of stone about three or four feet wide separating the opposite houses. It is most inconvenient to meet a sacred cow in the lanes of the city, for you must needs squeeze tightly to the wall; for the cow takes her pleasure, pokes her head into bazaars, opens doors and windows, and begs her food from house to house. It is a most meritorious act to feed the sacred cows; so they stray about the city at will.

Another temple still remains to be seen; and proceeding on our way, we soon find ourselves in the paradise of the descendants of the faithful Hanuman, Son of the Wind, the Rescuer of the precious Bride of Rama, whose legendary story runs something like this: It chanced once upon a time that this most mighty of apes volunteered to restore the long lost Sita to her sorrowing husband; and believing the beautiful woman to have been kidnapped by the King of Ceylon, he bids his simians to construct a bridge from India across the narrow sea. When this is finished, a command is given to cease; and the monkeys drop the mighty stones at that very moment. And even to this day a huge line of rocks continues from the Island of Lanka to the Himalaya Mountains. Hanuman then sweeps his tail, one thousand miles long, around the island, and then contracting it, finds Sita safe and sound with a dash of sunlight in her dreamy eyes. So the valiant Hanuman was elevated to a place in the Hindu heaven, and his descendants are beloved of gods and men.

We are advised not to enter the temple without providing ourselves with sweets and gram from the venders on the doorsteps, otherwise the apes would be disagreeable, perhaps dangerous. Once inside, we witness a curious spectacle: up come the monkeys in crowds, springing from the lovely green trees, bounding toward us from the temple pinnacles, unwinding their long tails from the carved marble pillars, climbing the surrounding walls above our heads, and reaching down for the contents of the trays. One old yellow monkey evidently thinks we do not give out the sugar things fast enough; and like a flash upsets the dish from our hands, scattering the grains on the floor, then picking them up with both hands and eating them. The priests are dirty and miserable, and demand "backsheesh" all in a clamor. This temple is extremely sacred in the eyes of Hindus, and crowds of worshippers come every day to strew flowers to the idol wife of Siva, the goddess Dunga. The white flowers of the temple, strung on threads, are put about your neck by the priests, and are extremely pretty. Flowers, white and yellow, float continually in rich masses of color on the river, and are carried in baskets to throw before the idols in temples and shrines. The Hindus, with whom the principal virtue consists in allowing the very nasty water of the Ganges to enter their mouths, and who wash themselves and afterwards their clothes in its waters, in devotion to Dunga, still have no idea of cleanliness. The streets are full of unusual scenes; sometimes a man squats by the gutter curb-stone brushing his teeth,—this I have seen.

Sunday, February 1.

I was glad this morning to go to an Episcopal Church-service in Benares, the old stronghold of Hinduism; and I wondered if it were more wonderful that the New Zealand traveller should in future years take his stony seat on London Bridge, than that an American girl should find her own church-service flourishing so naturally in the citadel of idolatry, the sacred Hindu city, where Buddha preached, convincing the thousands of Brahmins after his great renunciation. This is, however, a fulfilment of the law of progress, the order of things natural and things spiritual,—the stream of tendency which makes for righteousness.

February 4.

To-day we drove to the Bishishear, or Holy of Holies, the Golden Temple. It is reached through long twisted lanes, so narrow that two persons can scarcely pass side by side, lined with merchants sitting cross-legged, or in the Hindu manner perched beside their wares, like so many crows. They sell brass work, kincob embroideries, and idols and rosary beads. But the greatest traffic is with the idols,—stubby little fat gods on wheels or otherwise, brass or clay, small and great alike are displayed on the long shelves which front and line the shops. Here is a crowd of pilgrims making their bargains, and departing with their purchases wrapped up in a piece of brown paper. The favorite deity seems to be Ganesh, the shrewd and cunning elephant god, or perhaps Krishna, the frolicsome partner of the milkmaids. Few idols are ever sold of Brahma, the universal spirit, who at present, it is said, is only worshipped in two places in India. The work of creation finished, the Hindus prefer to devote their gifts and prayers to propitiate the two remaining "powers that be,"—the destroying Siva and Vishnu the preserver.

The Golden Temple is gold only so far as the sheathing of the pagoda pinnacles are concerned. Near by is the Well of Knowledge,—the place where Siva himself is said "to have had the bad taste to reside." It is a small square building, swarming with dirty fakirs and sleek Brahmins. Cows are straying about at will, and withered heaps of flowers strewn everywhere make the place, the air, and the surroundings almost unendurable. In former days the devout threw in the well offerings of coins, pice, and silver. The priests, in order to profit by these gifts, originally employed a diver, but now have dispensed with his services by roofing the well with copper in order to rake in the shekels more conveniently and surely; and so the poor deity, like Mother Hubbard's dog, "gets none." On leaving the temple the worshippers have a custom of sounding the huge bell suspended by a chain in every temple. After closely questioning our Hindu guide as to the meaning of this, he finally managed to explain it in this way, which I thought very amusing: "Sahib rings bell; that is to say, 'Good-by, Goddess, now I go; please excuse me all my sins.'"

At the Cow Temple we were only allowed to enter one step in the building,—quite enough we soon discovered. A more ridiculous sight one cannot imagine. Thirty cows are kept in the temple court; they walk about, poke their heads curiously into the most holy shrines of Siva, examine the carvings like connoisseurs, and the whole place is nothing less than an ill-kept stable. The place simply reeked with horrid smells, and was not improved by the crowd of fakirs and much-smeared beggars continually streaming in with purest gold wreaths of marigolds and whitest temple flowers to decorate the senseless, ugly idols. They all receive a mark from the Brahmin,—a sign that they have visited and performed devotions in the temple. It is generally a round dab of red paint, or white, just between the brows; and, in fact, we no longer notice the war-paint of the *religieux*, — it is so universal. Every man who worships Vishnu is painted with perpendicular streaks between the eyes. Siva's disciples are marked horizontally across the forehead. Married women all have a red painted mark where the hair parts in front, besides caste-marks. In this country the women wear huge nose-rings,—the Mahometans a gold stud merely on one side of the nose, which Rudyard Kipling says "takes the place of the Western patch" in drawing attention to the curve of the nostril; their ears are pierced with from two to twelve rings loaded with stones; armlets and bangles in heavy succession hide the arms; and anklets put on in childhood, which can never be taken off after, keep the ankles small.

We are told that January and February are the great months for rivers and the worship of the idols. The Hindu gods go to sleep in the hot season, when their temples are deserted. Now they have just waked up, and are ready to open court, as it were. Their chief god, Brahma, they believe is now in prison. He was so very bad that the other deities held a council and decreed to imprison him. The triune divinities are so unexceptionally bad that one cannot really blame the people for imitating them. Brahmin temples are not meant for large gatherings; they are small, containing only a shrine surrounded by an inclosed court. This is because the devout only come and stay a few minutes every day, offer something to the Brahmin attendant, ring a bell, and go away satisfied. No one has a right to pray or offer gifts directly to a deity; everything must be done through a Brahmin priest.

This morning we started out on the white dusty road in a palanquin-carriage for Sarnath, six miles from Benares, on the great high-road leading from Calcutta to Afghanistan and its border city, Peshawer. India is one great prairie, so level that from the coast hills to the Himalayas the country is a flat table-land. We see Sarnath afar off; a wonderful Buddhist relic it is,—a mound of bricks once covered with beautiful carving, of which pieces now exist, half hidden by the moss and grasses growing in the crevices of the tope. Here Buddha once preached, and from here the Buddhist monks have carried their religion over the East. For centuries the tope at Sarnath has been the most remarkable Buddhist monument remaining to India, for a strange fortune has made Brahminism hold the ancient city as a spiritual capital; and the lowest, the most idolatrous religion of priest worshippers has risen in the Faranase of Buddha, the contemporary of Nineveh and Babylon, the oldest city in the world.

CHAPTER X.

AT LUCKNOW AND CAWNPORE.

February 6.

IT is breezy. I am wearing my coat over a blue woollen frock. Lucknow now can feel cold, at least in contrast to the glare and heat of Benares. The trying part of this climate is its fickle thermometer, which early in the morning is very low, and gradually goes up until midsummer heat is reached at noon, only to scamper down again at sunset. We arrived last night at ten o'clock, and have seen nothing of the place or people, except the dhobie who came for my clothes this morning, and who looked as if a good laundry soaking would do his one dirty garment good. The process called "washing" in the East is not a costly affair. Four rupees is the price,—not per dozen, but per hundred. I have caught melancholy glimpses of enlightenment as to the original cause of unmendable rents, buttons demolished, and the general ruin which invariably ensues from confiding fine linen to the mercies of an Indian dhobie. At some unexpected sylvan riverside you come suddenly on a line of dusky forms, each bending violently forward, then backward, pounding some flapping vesture on the rough stones of the stream. I have copied the following written sign from my door-panel in the hotel,—a scale of rates which varies seldom, and may be said to be fairly characteristic of the best inns:—

Board and Lodging	5 rupees per day.
Indian servants, separate room	5 "
Native servants, food, per day	2 "
	4 annas quarter day.
Punkah-wallah, per day.	3 "
" " per night	3 "
Dhobie, per hundred	4 rupees.
Coolies to carry baggage to and from railway station	1 anna.
Stabling, per month	8 rupees.

Once in Lucknow, it goes without saying that you are at Hill's Hotel, —a queer affair indeed for a hotel: one long colonnaded veranda; behind that are our sleeping-rooms, only shut off from the grassless, sun-baked compound by an old, transparent, bamboo curtain, which barely hangs together outside a pair of doors always open, and which I have discovered will not lock. The house seems a quarter of a mile long by one room deep; there is no office or clerks or desk to be seen. You shout down the open piazza for paper and ink, and sooner or later a dusky figure occupies the perspective of the columned quarter mile of piazza, and produces them from somewhere. Hotel life in India is a system of shouting. Outside my door is a motley crowd of Afghans,—men from Kabul and Lahore, the Nimrods of Northern India,—who have brought their furry winter merchandise to palm off on the tourists now gathered on the wide veranda to spend the hours after tiffin, reclining in long bamboo chairs, with a semicircle of natives squatting behind knotted muslin bundles, ready at the least encouragement to produce anything in the taxidermist's line, from a Himalaya fox to a Bengal tiger. This is a great convenience. It is a shade cooler in your room, perhaps, and you have only to pull up the crackling curtain, and sit there beyond the heat and worry of the bazaars. A slight signal starts forward the whole pack, who lay their treasures at your feet; and without any trouble you judge and criticise, and then select an equivalent to the silver rupees thrown down on the floor, which are quickly transferred to the mass of dirty rags around the Afghan's waist, and pays his return journey to the snows.

February 7.

"Here lies Henry Lawrence,
Who tried to do his duty."

These two simple lines on the grave of the English general seem to sum up for all the brave men murdered in the Indian mutiny the most fitting expression and epitaph. The vine-covered ruins of the Residency stand sentinels over the graves of women and children and English heroes, once happy and free, who died ten thousand deaths before the end came in the terrible summer of the siege of Lucknow. Sir Henry Lawrence's dying words tell the simplicity and heroism of his life. Three English heroes have used the same expressions at life's end. Nelson's was, "Have done my duty;" Gordon's, likewise; and Sir Henry Lawrence said, modestly but eloquently, "Tried to do my duty." We drove to-day to the scenes of the mutiny. All will be impressed indelibly on my memory,—the Residency, the bailie guard-house, the churchyard, with the pink petals falling from English rose-bushes and covering English graves, and the loving vines creeping over all the ruins to hide the dreadful marks of sorrow and desolation. The great Borgan Villia flowers throw a purple curtain of mourning over the death-chamber in the Residency, where Sir Henry Lawrence died.

At the first symptoms that a revolt had broken out in India, Henry Lawrence, the Commissioner of Lucknow, summoned the little European colony scattered about the town to come in haste to the Residency for protection. On the 29th of June the native regiments of the fort went over with all their arms to the Sepoy mutineers, leaving only fifteen hundred soldiers, with several hundred women and children, to sustain during several months of an Indian summer the frail ramparts thrown up hastily around the Residency, against a terrible foe, ten times more numerous than themselves. One is awed and hushed into silence while walking through the scenes of that awful sorrow and suffering that came to these poor creatures in that improvised fortress. The pitted walls bear the traces of the explosion of shells and cannon-balls, which came with incessant rumblings from the rebel camp, just across the flower-gardens of the Residency, and mingled with the cries of the wounded and the moans of the weeping wives and mothers. The slightest exposure of the women and children at the windows was followed by a death-shot from a sharp-shooter. And all night long processions of mourning friends filed out under cover of the darkness to the little enclosure by the church, —which became that summer, in place of the smooth green lawn, a great mounded acre, till those who had "fought the good fight, and kept the faith," far outnumbered those still fighting. Towards the end of September every hope seemed lost. The assailants had gradually approached so near the place that only a few acres of the flower-planted lawn stretched between those desperate, brutal, leering faces and a handful of discouraged soldiers. Sir Henry Lawrence was dead, — struck by a shell in a moment of brave exposure to fire; but as news of his death would come as a shock to the already shattered hopes of the soldiers, no one had dared to mention it until days after. Cholera and varioloid each day carried off new victims, and then the provisions threatened famine; but the end had come. One day, the wife of a Scotch sergeant suddenly cried out that she heard in the distance the sound of a bagpipe, playing "The Campbells are coming." No doubt, every one thought she had gone mad, until the cannonading announced the approach of the invincible Highlanders. There was one moment of inability to realize the glorious deliverance; in the next, every one shouted and danced for joy, and wrung the hands of these great sun-burned men, and praised the Great Deliverer that the Campbells had come.

Mutiny days are still vividly remembered in India. Three soldiers were being driven in a cart by a native coachman toward Cawnpore soon after the mutiny. As they were nearing the city the native made a remark in Hindustani, of which the soldiers only understood the word "Cawnpore." This name uttered by the native struck such a tender cord of memory in the minds of the soldiers, that in a frenzy then and there they hanged the man to a tree by the roadside. The interest attached to the Residency at Lucknow completely overshadows all other desires in regard to sight-seeing.

The capital of Oude is called the City of Palaces. The architecture is a strange mixture of the Moorish and the Renaissance, more like French structures and the pink-and-white prettiness of the Cirque d'Hiver. In fact, we did not visit the imperial abodes at all. It was exasperating enough to drive by; and even to come in contact with them from the carriage window was unpleasant. A compilation of colonnades, of arches and minarets, a heaping up of domes surmounted by umbrellas, with a façade of confectionery, rejoice in the name of the Palace of Chantar Manzil. Another palace, "a little Louvre in stucco," forms an enormous square of ornamental plaster; it cost millions of money, and was the royal residence of the last king of Oude. It seems that the princes of Oude possessed a mania for building; and the result is a collection of palaces, gardens, tombs, and mosques, —bad examples of every style of architecture on the earth's surface. In the native quarter, you are in a true little Moorish city, with long, straight streets, low houses with grated windows, idols frescoed in fantastic colors on the Brahmin temples, and the descendants of mutinous Sepoys thronging their dirty streets. To reach the bazaars, you push on through narrow lanes, crowded with noisy natives, hammering away at copper vessels, tinkering at brass work,—the fires blazing, the odor of cooking penetrating everything,—the faithful reading the Koran, sitting cross-legged and unconcerned by all this bustle, confusion, and bewildering throngs of Cashmerian men, Persians, Bengalis, all crowded within a space of only a few feet, where our carriage seems to mow its way between the dark little holes of shops on either side.

But you have only begun to see the bazaars. From this one we pass on to others, full of strange interest. In another quarter men are pencilling on gold and silver the well-known jungle-pattern of feathery palms; rose-water bottles, cups and quaint boxes, trays and vases, all are decorated with this delicate design. An entire street is given over to the hookahs,—the *Suspira,* "the smoker's paradise," where you see a nargileh in silver, dainty enough to grace the apartment of a rannee, and also the more ordinary earthern "hubble-bubble" of the shopkeeper, who spends blissful hours every day in its company, looking like a bag of rags in a dark corner of the shop, his dirty white phoulkari drawn over his head, half asleep, and still unconsciously puffing away at the same time. What sights and sounds, and how alluring the place becomes as you go on to the artisan quarter and see the craft to which Lucknow owes its greatest fame! I have read a very accurate description, which says: "Gold and silver wire drawing, with its complementary trades of gold and silver lace, brocades, and embroidery, employs about one thousand artisans in Lucknow. The basis of these fabrics is gold, silver, or silver-gilt wire drawn out by hand—or rather by that extra hand possessed by every Indian, the foot—to an extreme thinness; sometimes used round, at other times flattened out into fine metal ribbons, or cut into spangles of various patterns: a rupee can be drawn out to eight hundred yards of wire. These products are far superior to anything of the kind produced in Europe by machinery; the wire is used largely in Ahmedabad, Benares, and indeed all over India in the manufacture of kincob brocades. The principal kinds of lace made at Lucknow from gold and silver wire are called *lachka*, *kalabatu*, and *lais*. In lachka, the warp is of silver-gilt strips, woven with a woof of silk; it is often stamped with patterns in high relief, and is mostly used for edging turbans and petticoats. Kalabatu consists of strips of gilded silver twisted spirally round threads of yellow silk, and then woven into a ribbon similar to lachka. In lais, the woof is of wire and the warp of silk. This industry reappears in the shoe and slipper bazaar, where beautiful embroidered velvet and leather slippers may be purchased. The native kings of Oude prohibited the embroidery of slippers with anything but pure gold wire, but the bazaars of Lucknow are now mainly filled with pinchbeck frauds from Delhi."

On the streets you meet hosts of women loitering, idling, and shopping, — wearing a drapery held together tightly to conceal the features, but often allowing the neck and shoulders to appear uncovered. These women are never occupied in the sales. The nation's shopkeepers are always men, disposing alike sweetmeats and furbelows, according to the inflexible customs of the East.

The greatest, the richest bazaar is left until the last,— the famous choak, or silver bazaar of Lucknow, where the native merchants sit in the open doors of their shops, with silver bangles and every sort of rough and fine jewelry spread out before them. The silver kings run out to our carriage, and smilingly salaam us an invitation to stop and buy. We step over the gutter running before the shop down the entire street, and perch upon the stone entrance, with our feet on the sidewalk. It is not a spacious shop, but the charm and novelty of it one can only find in the East. The stone platform just raised from the street a few feet, on which we sit, is literally carpeted with the silver jewelry in shining heaps, which is sold for the weight in rupees, with from six to eight annas additional, varying according to the fineness of the workmanship. The shop is only a few feet square, open to the air, and only large enough for the Hindu, ourselves, and the silver. Behind the platform is an unknown, dark, windowless region, in which Sham Lall keeps his treasures. It requires the patient spending of almost an hour to induce the man to show us his best work. All the ordinary wares do not entice us; so he finally disappears to his lair, and brings out of his strong box the delicate silver things that we see in Kensington Museum.

CAWNPORE, February 8.

Next day we take the Oude and Rohilkund Railway to Cawnpore, sacred to the memory of the mutiny, where your heart melts in pity for what was. A strange fascination for the horrible leads one to make a pilgrimage to General Wheeler's camp and the massacre Ghaut of Nana Sahib; and the following in a few words is what history has to tell of the deepest, darkest tragedy of modern times.

When the mutiny broke out, Sir Hugh Wheeler, who commanded Cawnpore, retired with seven hundred European men, women, children, and two hundred soldiers, into a couple of bungalows hastily fortified and armed with several cannon. Here at the Indian Thermopylæ, the Englishmen held in check thousands of rebels commanded by the rajah, Nana Sahib, who had tried for years to revenge himself on the British government. On the 26th of June, after twenty days of siege, the old general, dismayed by the decrease of food, was forced to listen to the proposition of the rajah, who assured him that his garrison would be allowed to retreat in safety from Cawnpore, the condition being a complete evacuation of the cantonment. The English hastily decided to take refuge at the fort of Allahabad; but they were scarcely embarked with their women and children in the boats that Nana Sahib had prepared for their journey down the Ganges, when a burst of artillery sounded from the shore, directed towards the little fleet, and all on board were thus violently precipitated into the water or instantly killed. Four men only escaped; the others swam ashore and were massacred, — or still worse, taken into captivity to prolong their agony a few days. On the 15th of July, an army, made desperate by the news of this terrible treachery, advanced on Cawnpore. Nana Sahib, believing himself lost, giving vent to his terrible despair and vengeance, calmly ordered the massacre of his prisoners of war. The men were immediately shot down; while the women suffered a more horrible fate, being confined in a narrow bungalow, and tortured by occasional levelling of the rebel guns at the windows through the roof. Afterward a band of Sepoys rushed into the building, cutting down the frightened women right and left, until maddened by terror they rushed out of the place, followed by the yelling Hindus. Seeing a well belonging to one of the pretty English villas of this ill-fated spot, they threw themselves in, preferring death in that way. Nana Sahib's men, closing in upon them, carried the dead bodies of the murdered women and threw them in with the living; and when the English soldiers came with relief twenty-four hours afterward, they found an unrecognizable, palpitating mass of human beings — the living and the dead — mingled together in that place. To-day the English have planted fragrant beds of roses and sweet English flowers about the scene of massacre; a reverential hush pervades the gardens, the trees and leaves rustle very gently, and the birds sing softly, — for the place whereon you stand is holy ground.

How fresh the memory of the mutiny still is in India! Everybody talks about it, and its horrors are in everybody's mouth. Such tales and happenings! Such misery! Miss S. told me to-day of the mysterious cakes sent to every native soldier before the mutiny, the meaning of which has never been explained to this day. A story is told of a family hiding in some chaff; when the Sepoys came up, they suspected something, and poking into the grain with swords, discovered the poor creatures, who were killed, all except a girl of seventeen years. She was released on condition that she would repeat the Mahometan creed, "Allah ho Akbar," which she almost unconsciously did. She was then delivered as a slave to the highest general, and sent to Mecca, where she was known by the name of Sara Begum. After twelve years in the harem, she sometimes came out and lived with Europeans for a little time, then returned to Delhi or Lahore, and became apparently a Mahometan again. No one knows who she was, and she refused to answer any questions, but insisted she still remained a Christian, and could do more good by abiding in the house of unbelief than returning to civilization.

CHAPTER XI.

AGRA AND THE TAJ MAHAL.

AGRA, February 10.

IT has been in the air for days. Floating bits of talk come to our ears, and they all repeat softly, almost reverently, "The Taj." For several days travellers have had an excited air; something is near, brooding over the future,—some great presence is about. Every one is hastening to the magnet, the climax, the glory of Agra; it seems the great pre-eminent and all-absorbing spot to which the whole creation of tourists move. So to-day, Sunday,—a true sun's day, bright, intensely bright and wondrously calm,—we visit the glorious tomb which Shah Jehan builded as a matchless monument to his love for Arjamand.

After three miles of dusty roads and dry, grassless fields, we reach the Jumna, and stop before a Moorish gateway, with white, dome-like crowns over the arches; and look! you stand breathless, with the Taj Mahal, hidden until now, before you. Through the tall archway stretches many feet of clear water, bubbling with fountains, and bordered by dark rows of cypress-trees leading straight up to the white marble, where from amid gardens of beautiful flowers and the surrounding green of shady trees rises lightly a great white blossom, a fragile, snowy lily, — the Taj. "You see it with the heart before the eyes have scope to gaze." High in air stands the ivory, creamy dream of white marble, — the magic of lines and arches, the unearthlike beauty of Arabic architecture. The slender cypress-trees in the foreground, the sunlight falling in bright patches of light on the rounded domes, the airy minarets all white and crystal, produce an exquisite effect against the deep-blue Indian sky. The thing which most impresses you is the whiteness; everything is purest marble. The inlaid work of precious stones, in garlands, sprigs, and rose-clusters, is the ancient model for all Florentine mosaic; and the entire Koran is inlaid in Persian characters over the Taj so smoothly that it looks like shadows on the marble. To say that inside and out the building is like a beautiful jewel-box would only half tell the story. Ah, how I could wish for Ruskin to tell me how to describe what I can only feel and dream, and thereby make the stones of Agra as dear to us as the stones of Venice! I could tell you that twenty thousand workmen took seventeen years to finish it, and still you would wonder how any earthly men could accomplish it in a single century, or ever succeed in doing it at all. I could tell you there is a garden all about the Taj, "where men sit and hear the bulbul singing to the rose, and talk of Arjamand and love and death." And you seek the stillness and repose of the winding paths and the acres of choicest flowers, and let them all come into your life, to sweeten and refresh it. It is true you get what inspiration you bring: come here in the mood for receiving good, and you find it; but you must be in sympathy with the hidden thought expressed in the marble, for a verse on the entrance says,—

"Only the pure in heart shall enter into the gardens of God."

To realize the deep sweetness of it all, to make you see the poetic lights and shadows, I quote Sir Edwin Arnold's perfect word-etching. Of the garden he says:—

"The garden helps the tomb, as the tomb dignifies the garden. It is such an orderly wilderness of rich vegetation as could only be had in Asia,—broad flags of banana belting the dark tangle of banyan and bamboo, with the white pavements gleaming crosswise through the verdure. Yet if the Taj rose amid sands of a dreary desert, the lovely edifice would beautify the waste, and turn it into a tender parable of the desolation of death and the power of love, which is stronger than death. You pace round the four sides of the milk-white monument, pausing to observe the glorious prospect over the Indian plains commanded from the platform on that face where Jumna washes the foot of the wall. Its magnitude astounds. The plinth of the Taj is over one hundred yards each way, and it lifts its golden pinnacle two hundred and forty-five feet into the sky. From a distance this lovely and aërial dome sits, therefore, above the horizon like a rounded cloud.

"And having paced about it, and saturated the mind with its extreme and irresistible loveliness, you enter reverently the burial-place of the princess Arjamand, to find the inner walls of the monument as much a marvel of subtle shadow and chastened light decked with delicate jewelry as the exterior was noble and simple. On the pure surface of this hall of death, and upon the columns, panels, and trellis-work of the marble screens surrounding the tomb, are patiently inlaid all sorts of graceful and elaborate embellishments,—flowers, leaves, berries, lapis-lazuli, nacre, onyx, turquoise, sardonyx, and even precious gems."

A truly wonderful echo can be heard in the interior. The sound of one's natural voice is taken up, lifted high in the dome from harmony to harmony, and like organ music swells grandly through the arches,—a beautiful effect of tones as if from a choir invisible; and in the centre of the snow-flower, deep in its marble heart, warm beams of sunlight fall through the lacy screen of alabaster on the tomb under the great dome, where lies Mumtaz-i-Mahal, chosen of the palace, and her royal husband, who willed all this beauty, and it was done. According to Mahometan custom, the real tomb is in a crypt directly below the false ones. It is said the great shah intended and planned a black marble Taj to be reared on the opposite bank of the Jumna, connected with this shrine by a bridge of silver; but the idea was abandoned, the shadow shrine never completed, and we are left to think that the princess who had so enchanted her royal lover willed it that he might, no longer living, belong to her forever,—for is she not Arjamand,

> "Thy own loved bride?
> The one, the chosen one, whose place
> In life or death is by thy side?"

To realize the fabled splendors of the "Arabian Nights," come to Agra, the city of the magnificent Akbar, who builded here a collection of the most glorious mosques, palaces, and musjids in the world, all of purest marble, surrounded by the walls of the fort as pearls are hidden within their dark enclosure. We enter the fort through the Delhi Gate; a roadway leads to a flight of steps, surmounted by the famous Moti Musjid, or pearl mosque, of which the guide relates that it was the private chapel of the Mogul emperor, and was built by Shah Jehan in 1654. At the first look you are dazzled by the brightness, as if the sun fell on a hill of snow far above, beneath, and all around you; pinnacles, roof, pavements, domes, and courts are all alike of whitest, stainless marble, carved, traced, and sometimes perforated like gauzy curtains between the window arches, the court shining like a crystal lake touched by sunbeams, where, in the centre, a fountain jets a diamond spray, and rows of exquisite pillars seem to attach this white cloud-structure to the earth, —

> "Without price, without flaw. And it lay on the azure
> Like a diadem dropped from an emperor's treasure;
> And the dome of pearl white and the pinnacles fleckless
> Flashed back to the light like the gems in a necklace."

When you long to think of something pure, when your sight is weary of the tortures of modern "high art" and artistic decorations, I can recommend you to close your eyes and see a refreshing vision of dome-covered arches, Saracenic pillars,—pure, spotless, colorless, "all white against a sapphire sky," —of which the inscription tells us that "it is truly a precious pearl, for no other mosque in the world is lined throughout with marble;" and nothing will make you see it better.

Now, this mosque is but a small part of the

treasures left to see inside the red tessellated walls. At first you cannot comprehend the vastness of the succession of Saracenic buildings. There is an open square farther on; cloisters surrounding three sides of it enclosing the great colonnaded Audience Hall, the Diwan-i-An of Shah Jehan, who built all these palaces, and here gave audience to his nobles, a rajah in attendance at every pillar; and if there were no other marvels, this one alone would repay you the journey.

Our guide conducts us by an exquisite stairway to the apartments of the Imperial Harem, — a bewildering vista of marble rooms, where dwelt all that was most lovely of womankind in the empire, protected from view by pierced marble screens carved like lace. A luxurious garden blossoms with roses and creeping vines; among them, in the olden time, fountains threw a perfumed spray and birds sang in the trees. A little distant was a fish-pond, once filled with gold-fish, where the rival beauties met, amused themselves, fished, and intrigued at the same time, no doubt for lack of other occupations. These fountains reflected Nourmahal, and perhaps the fair Arjamand, who, described as all sweetness, was nevertheless a bigot, and plotted the destruction of the newly-established Catholics; and jealousies, rivalries, and heart-breaks, mourning and laughing, went on all through the exits and entrances of the royal actors on this stage-land of state. In one courtyard has been laid out in marble blocks of gray and white a huge chessboard, where the Mogul king played chess with his sultana, with living chessmen, and just ordered the pages and little boy-knights to change about on the spaces. And we saw also, in marble, the royal game of parcheesi,—the same game, on a large scale, which we played as children. And the merry monarch Akbar had huge arched rooms, intertwining like a labyrinth, where he loved to see his little wives playing; and this is called the Palace of Hide-and-Seek.

The English government has set apart these wonderful palaces, which are just as fresh as the day the last workman left them, and keeps them protected from destruction. What would happen if a desperate war should be carried on in India? If you read of Akbar, who caused all this glory, you will see he was a wonderful man and most liberal in his views. A Mahometan himself, he nevertheless took a Brahmin wife from the Hindus; and he built for her a palace of exquisite Indian design, containing a temple for the idols. He also chose a bride from the Portuguese of Goa, a Christian girl, of whom he had heard through the Jesuits; and he built his Catholic wife a chapel with as many crosses as crescents.

We have only a few silent moments to imagine the life here as it was in the time of Persian splendor, for the guide will hold his peace no longer, and tells us that we must move on. In a moment more we are in the Diwan-i-Kass, and are listening to a statement that "the hall is sixty-four feet long and thirty-four broad, all of pietra dura;" and the fact is impressively declared that it is traced and chiselled, roof and mouldings, with lotus flowers and bud designs. How one would like to be quiet! but the guide now and then disappears altogether in the labyrinth of arches, doorways, and secret stairways; you give up the attempt, and only strive to keep in sight the Hindu's flying sashes.

St. John's College.

It was about twelve o'clock of the noonday when we first entered the compound of St. John's College, belonging to the London Missionary Society, where Indian boys are educated to pass examinations for the English universities, graduate, and receive degrees equal to the government colleges of India. We had voyaged down the Red Sea and through the Indian Ocean with the new rector, the Rev. Mr. H——, and he had promised on our arriving at Agra that we should see him and his college; and so one morning an Indian dog-cart drove recklessly around the narrow curves of Agra streets, and a wild Australian horse was jerked up at the steps of Laurie's, with the effect of nearly upsetting the rector. This was the first acquaintance of the English master with his steed, and the result was a complete misunderstanding. Terrified but brave, B. mounted the box-seat, I clung to the syce behind, and we whirled through the town, and with great luck landed "whole" at the college.

Seated in the portico at a long plain table were about twenty young natives, to whom a Brahmin pundit was giving a lesson. I questioned, and found it was Persian; and in the stone-floored central hall we afterward gravely inspected classes imbibing a comfortable amount of Arabic and Sanscrit, judging from the size of the volumes. We walked through the corridors also, where, divided into two separate rooms, were grown-up boys, who were learning pleasant moral maxims in English monosyllables from green primers. All the teachers and professors were pundits or muftis, wearing huge white turbans, and waxed fat and sleek from a generous stipend procured from parish collection-boxes over the sea; every student was dressed in embroidered and gilded garments, utterly unlike our college boys in all this finery, which looked most absurd when the boys were playing football and cricket. Many of the boys live in a plain, mud-thatched building in the grounds, and have over them a care-taker,—a dear old native, who is called a House-father. The floors of the house are stone, and the walls of their rooms clay. Like prison-cots, the low charpoys of the students were ranged along the side walls, standing about a foot from the ground. No other furniture was visible. The only attempt at ornament to be seen were the bright-colored pasteboard initials of the honor-men at English universities, that seemed to encourage the students to think there was some chance for them after all to go and do likewise. It was all so plain and bare,—a simplicity that Greek philosophers might have approved, and scarce fell short of the mark aimed at by the Jesuit colleges.

Like every one else who comes in contact with Indian missions, we revealed an amazing amount of latent interest in them, up to that moment scarcely suspected by ourselves. During the day the Rev. Mr. H—— related many interesting things in reference to the missions in Agra, and we listened eagerly while the rector talked about his college. There are four hundred natives being educated at St. John's College (only forty of them are Christians), and it is possible for a native to get his education with ordinary care for from eight to one hundred rupees. In the Church missionary boarding-schools the charge for students is eight annas a month. In competing with government schools, in which the charges are merely nominal, St. John's is obliged to offer very low terms. Putting missions on trial is a favorite amusement; but I think after hearing the case argued by the results in India, the percentage of people who would not give a verdict of admiration is very insignificant.

In the compound of the rector's bungalow there is a small building, occupied by seven Hindu and as many more Mahometan students. They have separate servants, who prepare the food; and they take their meals alone, squatting on the ground, and eating with their fingers. Among the students are several of the highest castes in India, and one boy is the descendant of the great Seyd. He is a noble fellow, tall and athletic, with a splendid head and great dignity of expression; and the rector told us that after years of study and intercourse this brave young Mussulman has become quite convinced of the errors of his inherited faith. When the reports on examinations were to be sent in to the Allahabad University, and each boy was asked to what creed he would be put down, Seyd, in spite of the derision of other students, and at the hazard of all his prospects to fortune and title, replied, "A Christian." So he has consented to become one on Sunday. The indignation among the natives is intense; the town is infuriated; nothing else is talked of. His mother says that this will break her heart, but his father declares he will kill him. Hoping to intimidate the missionaries, the Mahometans held a meeting last Sunday morning, at which they passed a resolution that, should the baptism take place, it be decreed that no Mahometan boy in future attend a Christian college.

The missionaries complain justly of the attitude of the British government of India toward the Christian religion. Any amount of toleration is shown to all other creeds. A Hindu may proselytize as much as he will; Mahometans may preach and make converts; but the Christian religion must not be spoken of in high places. In fulfilment of treaty conditions with the heathen, no government servant is allowed to attempt their conversion. No Bible history is taught in the government colleges everywhere established, but the works of Huxley, Schopenhauer, and other infidel literature is allowed. As an illustration, a commissioner of a certain province in India at one time took an active part in a Salvation Army meeting, which had gathered to explain some portion of Bible history to the soldiers. He was soon informed by government authority that he would have to give up his Bible class and meetings, or resign his post. I cannot give you all the details that I heard, but I recall scraps of the conversation. I soon discovered that the outcries of missionary failure in the West were as nothing to the complaints against nominal Christianity among English-speaking people in the East. The deadness of Anglo-Indians toward their church, the bad effect of their inconsistent lives and example, are declared by missionaries to be positive hindrances to their work. There is not even neutrality among the Anglo-Indians, but an absolute aggressive attitude towards Christianity; and the heathen simply cannot understand the difference between the lives led by the missionaries and those of the many foreign residents. A Hindu rannee once arrived at a most unflattering solution of the problem when she said, "You have people among the English that are not Christians, just as we have." All this and much more we heard that day; but there remains yet very much of Agra which clamors to be inked down in my journal.

February 11.

I shall remember long and well the evening spent at the rectory bungalow at Agra. There is not a more charming household in India, nor one where the mistress is kinder and more gracious to her guests. What a luxury it is to dine in a quiet house after two months of life in hotels, none but those who have experienced it can know.

During the evening a message was sent to the native students, who occupy a small bungalow just beyond the palm-trees, to join us. The dark-eyed Indians were soon seated in a long, uncomfortable, bashful row, in eight chairs pushed back straight along the opposite wall of the little drawing-room. I think the latent consciousness of superiority materializes when you come face to face with your dark-eyed brothers. One was a lad with a peculiarly high-bred look and a sweet and gentle face. His velvet embroidered clothes showed that he was of the upper class,—a Seyd of the family of Mahomet. The other boys were not less interesting; and they returned our glances from under their long lashes, as in our way we were quite as much "curios" to them as they to us. Silence followed,—an embarrassing silence. We knew not what to say to them; so at first said nothing, but took long looks at the rector's little melodeon that occupied the opposite corner from where those eight young heathen sat motionless, though they seemed to pervade the whole room. It was agonizing, this social contact of the races. We could go on well with guides and native shopkeepers, who, half Anglicized themselves, knew how to take us; but these undiluted heathen were not intelligible beings to us. We only knew that in their eyes we were committing a peculiar sin in merely sitting in the room with the sahibs. Has not Mahomet said, "Let your women be in seclusion"? and worse still, in our distant trip to Eastern countries, were we not disobeying the Tamil proverb taught by their mothers, which says, "Ignorance is an ornament to women," and which followed out, denies to their sisters changes of scene, while a superstitious religion seals the pleasures of such small social joys as these? To our relief, the rector suggests music; and B. gratefully takes the chair at the melodeon, and produces a fragment of Western song to a pagan audience. It is the "Last Night," and very well sung. If Western speech was as lead, Western song was as adamant to their comprehension. This old friend among songs heard every night in another land would never fail for applause; but the Indians understand nothing of the melody, and think the trills and scales wonderful but unnecessary; they sit strangely dumb, with their arms folded, and pay no tribute to the music. When two more selections meet the same fate, we retire; and after an interval the boys offer no objection to our request, and sing some native râgs in their own style,—a pensive, musical pace.

The musicians of India have a perfect scale of seven tones; they have composed a certain number of *râgs* (tunes), believed to be of divine origin, and the invention of new musical compositions or the least variation of those existing is forbidden by the priesthood. Quaint Oriental airs, full of weird melodies and strange effects of time and rhythm, are the gazals sung by the Mahometans of Northern India. Hindustani musical compositions, called Bhajans, are even more irregular and abrupt. The beginnings, endings, and erratic spirit of the tunes would not be condoned to Berlioz, to whom much musical eccentricity is forgiven. For illustration, I quote from the Hindustani "Tune Book," published at Lucknow:—

"A bhajan is composed of three parts: first, the prelude, which usually concludes with a repetition of its opening strain; then follows the air proper, consisting of two or four lines, these being repeated severally or otherwise; after which the refrain begins. This generally leads back to the latter part of the prelude, ending with its last strain. The second, as well as each succeeding verse, begins with the air and closes with the refrain."

Moderately fast.

PRELUDE AND REFRAIN. BHAJAN.

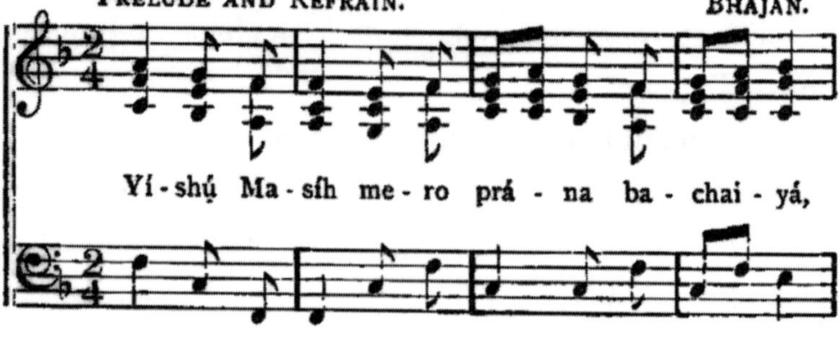

2. Yíshú Ma - | síh ki maiṉ | bali bali | jaihūṉ,
   Yíshú | hai mero | tràna ka - | raiyá.

3. Gahirí wuh | nadiyá | náwa pu - | rání ;
   Yíshú | hai mero | pára ka - | raiyá.

4. Día | nátha a - | nátha ke | bandhú ;
   Tuma hí | ho, Prabhu, | pápa ha - | raiyá.

5. Ási ko | apaní | sharana meṉ | rakhiyo ;
   Áṉta sa - | mai merí | líje ḳha - | bariyá.

[1] Sometimes sung thus

Gazals, sung in Urdu,—the language of Mahometans and of commerce, the French of India,—

generally consist of a prelude, air, and refrain. They naturally resemble Persian and Arabian models.

2. Maut kyá já - | ne larakpan | kyá burhápá | kyá jawáni,
Kyá amíri | kyá faqírí | maut ko par - | wah nahiṉ hai.

3. Kyá tirí áṉ - | khoṉ meṉ ab ták | níṉd gaflat | kí baṛí haí,
Bháí aur má - | dar pídar yáṉ | koí bhí ap - | ná nahíṉ hai.

4. Mál o daulat | shán o shaukat | in meṉ dhokhá | hai sarásar,
Sárí dunyá | koi kamáwe | tau bhi kuchh hásil | nahíṉ hai.

5. Hai shajar par | ḳhár dunyá | zindagání | hai kaháni,
Ġam alam má - | tam siwá koí | aura is meṉ | phal nahíṉ hai.

6. Hai mára rah - | mára dunyá | zahr qátil | se bharí hai,
Is ká káṭá | koí musáfir | eka dam jí - | tá nahíṉ hai.

7. Jaish o Jamshed | o Faredún | Bahman o Dá - | ra Sikandar,
Mil gae sab | ḳháka meṉ un | ká patá mil - | tá nahíṉ hai.

8. Hai ḳhushí I - | sa Masih meṉ | ráha haqq Sá - | bir wuhí hai,
Kyúṉ phire bhaṭ - | ká musáfir, | aur to koí | ráh nahíṉ hai.

A musician has said that these mournful, unsatisfied, expectant endings give us a clew to the minds of the people of India. From the very first note the immovable Asiatics preserved the peculiar, impassive, and devotional expression of face as if performing a religious rite; and indeed no one could be indifferent to the beauties of the venerable Vedic tunes, which seem in their strangeness to reach back to the reeds of Jubal or to their own Krishna fluting to his maids. As the conch-shell holds forever the murmur of the sea where it was born, so the wind-voiced music of India retains its birthright, — the rhymes of Nature, for whose worship it was created. The palm-whispers of her forests, the cry of her famines, the scorched Asoka blossoms withering on the dead earth, breathed a pathos into every note of the music.

> "'T was not the air, 't was not the words,
> But that deep magic in the chords,
> And in the lips that gave such power."

And we were like Salim, who, listening to Nourmahal's enchanting song, had lain —

> "Some moments rapt as in a trance,
> After the fairy sounds were o'er,
> Too inly touched for utterance,
> Now motioned with his hand for more."

I think we spent the greater part of that evening "motioning for more," until the boys finally grew weary, and we invoked the rector to express our pleasure; and I dare say, from the delighted expression of the singers, it was very neatly and creditably done. And so, raising the right hand, the students salaamed their host, and said good-night in the Eastern fashion, which was probably something like this: "The humble slave of your Gracious Majesty considers it an honor to cross the threshold of his palatial dwelling;" to which the rector inclines his head profoundly and replies, "The servant of your Gracious Lordship is most grateful for the honor of entertaining the most noble lords in his miserable hut;" and we also arise and say our regret at leaving with much more truth than usually slips into the Western speech of the *mem-logs* (white ladies).

CHAPTER XII.

AT FUTTEHPORE SIKRI.

February 12.

HOW nearly we lost Futtehpore, that loveliest of places! How few travellers visit it! but it is not perhaps the less worthy on that account. The drive to Futtehpore Sikri takes three hours and a half. Relays of horses are stationed at intervals of six miles on the road, where we were always greeted by packs of children, coming apparently out of the ground, for no dwellings, mud-huts, or other habitations were to be seen, — thin, undeveloped, half-dressed children, who first satisfied their curiosity about our clothes, and then whined for backsheesh as loudly as their poor little throats would let them. But as this goes on all day, nobody minds it; and it did not in the least disturb the remarks of our *vis-à-vis*, the rector, who entertained us during the drive by telling stories of native character. Among other things he told us that "in the interior of India there exists a people called Thugs,—a separate caste who worship Kali, the fearful wife of Siva, a furious goddess, hideous in features, with a necklace of human skulls smeared with blood. She is the patroness of the Thugs, who travel about the country committing crimes in her honor. An inhabitant who wishes to secure his house from robbery goes to one of the brigands and says, 'Now, look here; I will pay you two rupees a month, and I expect you to see to it that my goods are not stolen.' This puts the Thug on his mettle; and if anything happens during the month to disturb your peace, you just go to your man, and he, knowing well the members of his caste, will at once find out the thief and restore your property,—all of which seems to suggest that the old saying, 'Set a thief to catch a thief,' originated in the country of the Thugs."

In the Hindustani language there seems to be no word corresponding to honor. On all sides we hear complaints and outcries at the chronic state of dishonesty among domestic servants. There is no doubt about it, they will all cheat you right and left; and one learns to accept this state of things as a necessary condition of Indian life. In proof of this, I remember that an Anglo-Indian lady, who might be trusted to state the facts very fairly, and who I thought had great cause for bemoaning this state of things, once told me that when her kansamah presents his bill of monthly expenditures at the bazaars, or markets, she merely glances at the account; and if the sum is fifty rupees, she reckons at once that thirty-five rupees is the correct amount, and offers it to her butler, who, well knowing that it is right, receives it very contentedly. As for keeping a cow in India and enjoying the luxury of fresh milk, this is not to be thought of. Your servant would always assure you that yours was a very bad cow, and did not give any milk, in order to force you to buy from the milkmen, for the sake of a commission; and on every article which comes into your house you pay a price which includes the servant's commission of four annas. Another lady told us that her domestics insist that the hens do not lay eggs; and then immediately produce a basket, which she pays for, knowing well she is buying the very eggs her own fowls have laid.

On arriving at Futtehpore, our guide, according to his own statement, was a nephew of the old custodian of the place, a descendant of the prophet Jacob and of Sheik Salim Chisti, the favorite and saint of Akbar's time, whose family have lived here for three hundred years. Futtehpore Sikri is a city of palaces, a well-preserved mass of the finest style of Hindu and Mahometan architecture, built entirely of the ruddy sandstone which resists so well the effect of time and climate. It is said that the palaces, temples, shrines, and carved colonnades, which in Akbar's time covered over two square miles, were only occupied for fifty years, and then deserted at the bidding of the Moslem saint, Salim Chisti; but one would much more readily believe it was the stagnant water that drove the court to Agra.

This pleasure-city covers the only high spot for miles. There is one flat plain stretching from Agra to Futtehpore Sikri, which we approach through an avenue of fine trees. Below the walls are level plains like the Roman Campagna; there is the same aspect of dry, grassy turf, through which stretch white roads, which grow fainter and gradually disappear in the distance. A few ruins of red sandstone arches break the view here and there, like the remains of the old Roman aqueducts. The people in the little village lie about the streets, and sleep away the sunny hours, which has a decided flavor of *dolce far niente;* while a still greater resemblance exists in the abundance of little insects in the village itself, filthy to the last degree, and odorous.

The history of Akbar, the founder of Futtehpore, is so entangled in tradition, in mystery and unreality, that it is bewildering. The Great Mogul was the first of the Tartars to behave himself like a Persian sovereign. He was a contemporary of Queen Elizabeth, liberal, but showing at the same time the Tartar nature of his ancestor, Genghis Khan; personally the very flower of his age, handsome, skilled as a workman, and so courageous that it is said he would spring on the back of a young elephant who had killed his keeper, and compel it to do his bidding. In religion he was a liberal, indulging in wine; neither a Mahometan nor yet a Hindu or a sun-worshipper, he tolerated all creeds and isms; and for a time even the Jesuit missionaries imagined they had converted the Great Mogul. At last, however, the seductive flattery of his Moslem wives gained the day, and Akbar was induced to believe himself the "Lord of the Period," and equal to the Prophet himself. Next, the wily minister Abdul Fayel would have him deified; and every morning from a palace window he presented himself for adoration as the incarnate Krishna, "a ray of the sun's rays." Then he died; and at Secundra his body lies in the noblest mausoleum in all India.

You enter the courts, passing under a high gateway, — the Bouland Dar Wage, — a triumphal arch, on which are inscribed the conquests of the "Shadow of God," Jubal-udin-Mohund Kham, the emperor, which dates about 1610 A. D. On the reverse of the entrance-gate is a verse, which after the manner of guides is translated for us in a musical utterance of misfit words, and being interpreted, reads: "Jesus, on whom be peace, said, 'The world is a bridge; pass over it, but build no house there: he who hopeth for an hour may hope for eternity. The world lasts but an hour, spend it in devotion; the rest is unseen.'"

But I like most the fine tomb of the holy fakir Salim; but which is the more remarkable, the great white mosque in the centre of the marble cloisters, or the delicate workmanship and lace-carved marble panels of the saint's shrine? It would require more than a day to see it all. The house of Birloul, the Hindu favorite of the emperor, whose dwelling has been compared to the mansion of a Cyclops, passed through the hands of a Chinese sculptor and the treasury,—a labyrinth, where tradition says Akbar played hide-and-seek with his merry wives; and then the Panch Mahal, or five-storied pavilion, built entirely of massive red sandstone, the capitals varying in design,—the one the guide pointed out was an original decoration, representing intertwining elephants' tusks; but after all I can only give the merest hint of it.

Suddenly the two natives appear on the top of the tessellated walls, and jump into a large open well eighty feet below. The water was covered with a thick, malarious slime, a large hole being cut in it where the divers struck the water; and they were as green as bull-frogs when they left the pool, and came sputtering toward us for rupees. They pleaded in vain for an encore of the proceeding. How I dislike to see people thoughtlessly and stupidly risk a broken neck! Returning to Agra, we became discoursive again. This time it is Indian politics.

"A conqueror is never popular even when governing under the name of Reform. The miracle of this age is the holding of India by the English,—about one hundred thousand troops against native artillerists, gunners, etc.," argued the Americans.

"But," asked the English, "were the Hindus ever better off in schools, in the administration of just laws, in newspapers? And then how about the native Indian Congress?"

"But," I replied, "do you suppose the native is grateful for all these things? Have you heard the story which occurs to me just now? A very poor and wretched native and an Englishwoman were once stopping before a half-ruined mosque on the roadside to Secundra, and after some talk between them, the native said, 'You English cannot give us anything so beautiful.' 'No,' said the woman; 'but then we give you bridges, good roads, good government, and railway trains.' But the native answered very seriously, 'It is worth three days of hunger to see a thing like this.'"

Then followed a general agreement from all sides that the English, while professing not to uphold caste, have themselves founded a new one, by refusing to meet the natives on an equal footing, except in the civil offices and the street cars; and that even the Eurasians are made to suffer from this hauteur of the English towards the national aristocracy.

And thus the talk ran on until we reached Agra.

CHAPTER XIII.

DELHI AND ITS RUINS.

February 13.

WE have passed over the Jumna, and the train has stopped at Delhi, known as Shah Jehanabad, or the City of Shah Jehan, he who builded more lavishly and splendidly than any other man that ever lived. Now, as in old days, Delhi is surrounded by a tessellated wall, enclosing a city of domes and towers, of minarets and temples, half visible through the dense foliage of acacia-trees. Delhi was never a great city under the Mahometans. Talboys Wheeler says that "it was a camp turned into a capital. There were broad streets and narrow lanes, but the bulk of the houses were mud huts, little better than common tents; and even the mansions of the grandees, with their imposing gateways and courtyards, were mostly built of clay, whitened with lime. The Mahometan courtiers, whether Persians or Turks, were creatures of a day; their wealth depended solely on favor with the sultan. They had no landed estates; but the princes of Rajputana, who dwelt at court, built the great palaces of Agra and Delhi, and built them for all time."

North-Brook Hotel is close beside the old city wall; and sometimes in the late afternoon we walk through a lane, formed by its stony sides, to the modern town, pass in the yellow sunset caravans of camels, each one tied by the tail to the head-stall of the camel behind, all in single file, their long necks undulating, sometimes stretched high in air to pull off the green branches of the trees. In some places in the East it is customary to harness a pair of camels to a London mail-phaeton. I wonder if this will be the next fad at Windsor Castle, imported along with Hindustani servants and Indian maharajahs. The *devoirs* of these beasts have a wide range,—serving cavalry regiments, for post-office delivery, hauling rails for the iron roads, often yoked with a bullock before the plough at a decided loss of the camel's dignity. So they serve in many ways and many works; but they have their play-day in the rainy season. Then, according to our native guide, "camels no work can, stay down in mud with roads;" which being interpreted means that the lengthy limbs of the "ship of the desert" can only be navigated in fair weather.

Often we spend an entire day with the Delhi shopkeepers,—insinuating, dark-eyed men, who are models of patience and perseverance. In sea-green cap, with pink sleeves under a gold-embroidered jacket, as I am writing Chotey Lall is sitting on the floor in our room, doing up in a muslin bundle his brilliant heap of cashmeres, Kutch silver, and embroideries, which we have inspected for the fourth time to-day. Chotey is a rich and famous merchant, whose "curios" and Indian jewelry are recommended by the advertisement card to have the double good fortune of being "under the distinguished patronage of His Royal Highness, the Duke of Connaught, and always in stock,"—two titles to British favor. This distinction does not deter him from running after our carriage, pointing out the well-thumbed name of Lady Jersey in his open book, who therein inscribes herself "satisfied with goods purchased."

By this time we know all the jewellers of Delhi, and are known of them. We have had five seated before us to-day, and many others outside the room, "who only stand and wait" their chance,—Moote Ram, and Chrisum Chund, and Hugi Mull, and other Mulls and Dasses and Rams, all polite and unruffled under sharp orders from Shanker to "clear out," "who told you to come in?" "do go," etc.; but the ebony tempters placidly unfold rubies and precious stones as undauntedly as before. "Be still, pack up your bundle, jow!" we cry, exasperated. They reply collectively, a well-feigned disappointment written all over their faces, "I am sorry you not buy anything from me," and generally press you "not to buy, only see;" and then the bargain begins. "What 'll you take for that pin?"—a bar of half-a-dozen light sapphires. "Asking price fifty rupees, selling price thirty-five rupees," replies this self-convicted extortioner; and the handsome eyes look very honestly in your face. "Believe my word, Mem Sahib, that my cost price." Now is the time to be utterly indifferent, telling him quietly that twenty rupees is your last word; and repeat very strongly, "Well, if you will not take my offer, go!" Ram deliberately packs, and ties up the muslin sheet used for transporting the wares from the shop, pausing frequently to discover any signs of your relenting; and at the end, if you hold out, he says, infallibly, and without emotion, two words,—"Take it." No more,—you have concluded the affair. The boy Shanker told us to-day that the customary fee to a private servant is two pice on each rupee, besides which each shopkeeper pays a commission of fifty rupees yearly to the hotel for the privilege of conducting these transactions.

Although nearly a week in Delhi, and almost in sight of the Chandni Choak, three of Eve's descendants have so far resisted the glitter and glamor of the alluring jewelry bazaars. This is quite enough triumph. There is no question of holding out another day. Sundry curious necklaces of Indian design handed about the parlors last evening after *table d'hôte*, and declared by their owners to be "great bargains," have made this impossible. Shanker is forthwith despatched for a suitable conveyance; and rushes wildly toward us, followed by a rather shabby little slatted box on wheels, with "No. 1" painted conspicuously on the door-panels, — a necessary precaution, to distinguish it from its poor relation, the second-class gharri. Between us and that little carriage is a crowd of tradesmen, conjured up by our appearance at the door of the hotel, each holding high his card and pressing it into our hands, and every one speaking broken English in a chorus: "Miss Sahib, you come to my shop; I am very cheap man, I not want to make profit; I have very good curiosities to show you;" and even after we were fairly seated the horses could not move, so great was the throng of them. "Chalo! juldi! jow!" or any other Hindustani phrases, however peremptory, had no effect. The superstitious creatures finally play their great card, running after our carriage with several articles in their hands, entreating, "Mem Sahib, make bargain, make offer, morning time, want to sell something;" or, when night comes, "Don't sell anything to-day; how much you give?" Every day there is the same ordeal to be passed, with additions; and at last they ride on the steps of your carriage, and order your gharri-wallah to stop before their shops when driving by them.

Our syce took us by devious ways through the alluring and fascinating streets of the Chandni Choak and silver bazaar. We suspect he well knew there is a limit to every tourist's resistance to temptation, and we would reach ours among the jewels of the Choak; so it proved. They all have an exaggerated idea of our requirements, and insist on showing us jewelry which we have not the slightest idea of buying. We lingered hours before these glittering things, whose owners said in such a beseeching way, "Don't buy, only look;" and the cunning Hindu outside rested his horses and himself, and contemplated placidly the amount of rupees he would snugly tuck away that night in the white folds of his native drapery as a result of the multiplication by hours of two rupees, the rate of carriage hire. We ended by leaving it all. It is strange that at first you meant to buy everything, but the more you look at the *santoshás*, "contentments," as the native ladies call them, the more you find a satiated feeling taking the place of first enthusiasm; and what you formerly coveted, you would now refuse at any price. And so, half an hour later that day, we were wandering through the great Imperial Palace of the Moguls, on the Jumna.

We have seen nothing in India so beautiful as this building. You enter through the Lahore Gate, made of massive red sandstone like the walls and towers, forming a vaulted hall three hundred and seventy-five feet long, and said to be "the noblest entrance known to any existing palace," presenting very much the effect of a gigantic Gothic cathedral. So far as the eye can see, lofty sandstone walls enclose an area over one thousand feet long by five hundred wide, covered with splendid musjids, silvery minarets, and lovely outlines of domes and marble columns. There are clusters of military barracks here and there, open squares, bronze rows of captured cannon, inscribed with English victories; for now the red-coated soldiers are quartered among the most splendid monuments of a fallen power.

We go first to the Diwan-i-An, an audience hall of polished marble glistening with inlaid work of precious stones, which leads to the Moti Musjid, the baths, and the zenana. But the chief wonder is still unseen. It is the Diwan-i-Kass, the private hall of audience,—and, as it were, the very jewel in the lotus among the buildings in the fort. It is also of white marble, exquisitely sculptured; and the long lines of columns, ornamented on the marble with gold and colors in flower-clusters, are quite new to us and our ideas. The designs are like the ceiling, which our guide tells us was once plated with silver; as if Shah Jehan had drawn up the contract with the obliging Genie, whom Aladdin summoned to build him a palace worthy to receive the Princess Buddir. Genie commands the lucky son of the Chinese tailor: "Let its material be made of nothing less than porphyry, jasper, agate, lapis-lazuli, and the finest marble; let its walls be of massive gold and silver bricks, laid alternately, so they shall exceed everything of the kind ever seen in the world." And indeed this palace so far answers to this description that you can read over the Moorish arches a gilded inscription in Persian: "If there be an elysium on earth, it is this, — it is this." Here was the peacock throne, whose fabulous cost never fails to reward the guide with little exclamations of "oh's" and "ah's" from the tourist, who can as a rule appreciate plain figures if not the subtle sentiment of the Taj. Nothing I can say about it will not be better said by the guide-book: "In the centre of this hall stands a white marble dais, on which was once placed the once-famous peacock throne, — a seat between the peacocks, whose spread tails were encrusted with sapphires, diamonds, rubies, emeralds, and other precious stones, in imitation of natural cocks. Over the back was a parrot, said to have been carved from a single emerald. This throne is reputed to have cost three millions sterling."

Our guide leads us to the Rung Mahal. Everywhere are arabesque screens pierced like lace; one of them is matchless in all India,—a cobweb in marble. The zenana and children's play-ground recall memory of fairy tales, — latticed and gilded, splendid with extravagant fancies, where rose-water played through marble fountains, scattering spray over the little princes; in a word, the refinement of Saracenic and barbaric splendor in the East.

CHAPTER XIV.

A WELSH RAREBIT.

DELHI, February 14.

SHANKER is setting our lunch-table; for we have deserted the *table d'hôte,* and dine in our apartments,—which is much too lofty a name, however, for a sitting-room and two stone-floored dressing-rooms adjoining, which sounds rather well; but, alas! the side walls have scarcely any white-wash where it ought to be, the "water-supply" is conspicuous by its absence, and a plain iron cot, made presentable by our travelling-rugs, harmonizes with the other appointments of the "best accommodations" at North-Brook's.

But to return to the luncheon. Our table has a centre decoration of some glorious greenish oranges, bought on our journey, arranged with bright leaves. The fruit, grown at Lahore, very much resembles mandarins, but is larger and sweeter, and covered with a thick, loose skin. The substantial part of the meal included chops, brought in on a gridiron having four iron legs, and several grooves converging towards a centre, on which the meat sizzles, hot and smoking. This is an original manner of serving hot meat at table, bridging over one difficulty lying in the culinary path of housekeepers. Our next dish is one which has shown no signs of scarcity since we reached India,—the ever present chicken, or "sudden death," as it is called here, from the Anglo-Indian custom of cooking a fowl that has been running about the garden half an hour before. Next, we have bread and jam,—the inevitable jam of the Anglo-Indians; and all I can say for the accompanying bread is that it is baked on hot coals, and only once in an age a miracle occurs which turns native dough into good bread. The butter made of the milk which comes from the buffalo is thin and blue, and tastes like ham. The most aggravating deprivation to condone is ice; but that is a luxury still unrepresented in Delhi. On the whole, the Indian cookery, unvaried and monotonous, is redeemed by the chutneys and chillies, which appear to be the spice of life in place of variety.

This tiffin was the type of all succeeding ones in Delhi,—a gastronomic experience occurring three times a day, proving that civilized man cannot only live without civilized cooking, but even become ecstatic over the country where he submits to it. A traveller usually arrives sooner or later at a fine contempt for what he shall eat, and a cheerful one as to what he shall put on.

This week has ended in our making one grand excursion to the Kootub,—the highest pillar in the world. Thus far we have strayed on the very brink of adventure, and circumstances have never favored a fall in the stream. I have thought many times, how shall I be forgiven the lack of hair-breadth escapes; how account for the absence in my journal of thrilling tiger stories in Indian jungles; how appease the expectations of those who wished me a safe journey, and at the same time held a strong opinion that my return might resemble the young lady from Niger, "who smiled as she rode on the tiger; and when she returned from that ride, the girl was inside, and the smile on the face of the tiger." We were a long time making up our minds if it were wise to venture a twenty-two mile drive in the noon-day heat and sun, but determined to take the risk,—an adventure at last; and B. suggested that we take the tiffin-basket and make a Welsh rarebit under the Kootub. The proposition was inspired, and awoke in us a sudden hunger. Half an hour later we set out in good form.

The railway station is the general provision-shop of Delhi for anything besides native fare; and with feelings of profound contentment we stopped

RUINS OF TEMPLE NEAR KOOTUB.

the carriage in passing, and bought the necessary ingredients for a good rarebit,—fresh cheese, and a pale green bottle labelled "Very light Bass's ale, bottled especially for India." Next, we turned through the narrow streets, making our way slowly, almost hopelessly, through herds of natives utterly unmindful of us and without curiosity, not even deigning to get out of our way. Passing the city gates, we found ourselves in the grand open country, interminable and impressive; but we were most thankful for the quiet in contrast to the "hum of busy cities."

Modern Delhi is surrounded for thirty square miles by the crumbling remains of seven cities. The beautiful mosques and palaces are half in ruins, but still give a fair idea of the ancient days, as almost every inch of roadway is bordered by the ruins of older cities; for Hindus, Afghans, Tartars, and Mahometans have in turn disputed the possession of marble Delhi. Now it is a pure Mussulman city; and the Empress of India has more sons of the Prophet to do her homage than has the sultan. What prodigals of extravagance were the Moguls! — "splendid spendthrifts," as some one has called them. It is not possible to conceive the lavish sums spent on these famous residences of the emperors, marble zenanas, the baths, the mausoleums, embroidered arches, curves, lines,—a page from the "Thousand and One Nights;" and it was only yesterday that this scene was peopled by these Moguls,—not like the pyramids, far down in the beginning of history, but yesterday, in our time almost. The road is wide, shaded continuously.

Humayoon, the father of Akbar, who inherited Hindustan, is buried in a magnificent tomb, half-way between Delhi and Kootub, which tomb is a sketch in sandstone of his marble palace in Delhi, where he met his fate. One evening, having ascended to the roof to say his prayers, his foot slipped, and he fell lifeless on the pavement below.

What a love of luxury and magnificence is shown by the descendants of Mahmood Gazna, who plundered the temples of the Rajputs, and converted them to the religion of the Koran. An hour later we sighted the Kootub's minar, towering two hundred and thirty-eight feet in height. It is divided into five stories consisting of convex flutings, each story finished by a carved gallery, and the whole structure embroidered with verses from the Koran and designs of arabesque work. The guide-book supposes it to be the most perfect tower in the world, and declares its carvings to be as fresh as though they were of yesterday's date, though it is six hundred and fifty years since it was begun by Kootub-ud-din in the latter part of the twelfth century, and finally completed by Altmish, his successor, about 1210 A. D.; and it has looked down on an unbroken Mahometan sway until the Mutiny, in 1857. Going on, you pass the old Hindu fortress of Lalkot in ruins, but still massive and imposing. Mosques and palaces of Hindu and Mahometan architecture, injured by Saracenic invaders, show traces of wonderful carving in an indescribable variety of friezes, capitals, and columns. Close by stands the tower of Altmish,—the most beautiful monument I have seen in India, and also the oldest. In the centre of this mosque is a curious iron pillar, standing twenty-two feet above the ground; no doubt the guide was right in saying, "It was erected by one Rajah Bhara to commemorate the defeat of the Bahilkas, near the seven mouths of the Indus, in 360 A. D." Much more astonishing is the fact that the ancient Hindus could forge a pure iron bar, heavier than any that has been forged until our time. What pleased me most were the inscriptions in Sanscrit, which I traced with my finger, keeping in mind the thought that Bhara's workmen who hammered the letters little thought that their skill would be preserved and guarded by a conqueror who was neither Persian nor Tartar, but the British Lion.

Here, under the shadows of Saracenic arches, where in their time of glory no infidel would have been permitted to take a step, now nestles under some lovely trees, close by the beautiful Kootub, a little thatch-roofed bungalow; and here we made our Welsh rarebit. In a few minutes the basket was unpacked, and the lunch spread on the piazza, protected from the sun and dust by bamboo curtains.

How do you think we supplied the place of the chafing-dish to cook the cheese? The natives cook on the ground, in a clay heap scooped out to hold a few charcoals. They use earthernware pots, and brass platters; and going into a native cook-house means such a revelation of dirt and uncleanliness that no recovery following a first visit has ever been recorded. So, plainly, we could not venture to cook the cheese *à la native.* After much discussion with our guide, he brought us a tin sheet with hot coals; and here in the excitement of the moment B. and I, on our knees, began to stir the mixture in our sauce-pan, while the smoke curled towards the Indian sky, and lurid flames lit up the faces of our audience. We had a crowd of native servants watching the operations, and had a strong suspicion that our cooking very much lowered our dignity in their eyes. They looked on wonderingly, not understanding how a European could voluntarily choose to work if his servant were there to do it for him; and I fancy they thought it had to do with some incantation or religious ceremony peculiar to our caste. But how good it all was after the struggle! and it is reasonable to suppose the like of it was never seen in this neighborhood, in Akbar's time or since. You are thinking, perhaps, that you can read the history of Delhi in books; but no one has written the story of a Welsh rarebit among the pleasure palaces of the great Moguls.

February 16.

The Nautch dance which we saw last evening was something like this. The kansamah of North-Brook's Hotel, knowing something of the tourist nature and sight-seeing propensities, has succeeded in exciting the curiosity of several "globe trotters" to witness a Nautch dance. He extolled the perfections of the Maharajah's dancing-girls, and informs us that the entertainment will cost each member of the party fifteen rupees. This explanation is perfectly satisfactory to every one, and especially to the kansamah, who will pocket, after the entertainment, a year's salary from the remaining rupees.

A Delhi Nautch dance means something new and novel even for India; so we joined the party which left the hotel at nine o'clock. Leaving the gharri at a certain point, we followed our servant, who holds a lantern to light our footsteps, about a quarter of a mile through the narrow lanes of the native town. Stopping before a low and rather mean appearing house, we entered a room where ten or more persons were sitting about in groups on the floor, smoking hookahs. We filed past these dusky figures, half hidden by the smoke, to our place of honor,—a slightly raised daïs arched off the room. The apartment was small, and covered by a canvas carpet very much soiled by muddy feet. Many lamps of different designs—old lamps and new lamps, rusty lamps and dingy lamps—hung from the ceiling. The wall was decorated with highly colored advertisement cards and very ancient English chromos, brought with great audacity in close relations with verses from the Koran. It is altogether the most primitive amusement hall one could imagine, but the more interesting on that account.

The entertainment was opened at once by a native handing us bunches of roses tied with fresh grasses, which he passed on a large tray. This was followed up by frequent offerings of confectionery of the native sort, which we politely tasted in a moment of courage, and then regretted. All this time the robing of the Nautch girls for the performance was going on quite informally before our eyes, no drop-curtain being dreamed

NAUTCH GIRLS.

of; and I amused myself by studying their strange ornaments and fanciful dresses, and, above all, revelling in the delight of something absolutely fresh,—a scene unhinted and undescribed by brush or pencil, at least so far as my experience goes. Everybody in the room except the audience was sitting on the floor, huddled together. One or two of the girls were finishing their evening meal, or smoking their after-dinner hookah.

The extraordinary simplicity of the entertainment which now began was only to be equalled by the serious dignity in which it was conducted. Three natives proceed with the orchestral prelude. One instrument was the Indian for banjo. Another man held two halves of a drum, fastened by a sash around his waist; these he pounded with his wrist, and slapped vigorously with the palm of his hand. The third man in the trio had a steel cup in one hand, and struck it furiously with another small cup in time to the beating of the drums. This musician was quite imposing enough to be a drum-major, or "Der Trumpeter von Saxingen." It was very amusing to see a baby toy in the hands of this superb, full-grown man. The tune was to me what Wagner might have been to these very musicians,—something expressive of ideas outside the realm of my musical knowledge. Very deliberately, entirely *sans façon*, from a group in the half unearthly atmosphere, a girl arose and came towards us with an indifferent air and the remains of her dinner still rolling around under her tongue. This young woman was really quite pretty, her slight figure undulating slowly with every step. Her dress has long red sleeves studded with jewels, flowers, and precious stones; a full skirt falls to her anklets. The sweetest little bare feet just peeped from under the golden pleats of her skirt, and the little brown toes have each a gold hoop, which did not look bizarre, but neat and effective. She wore a graceful tulle veil, draped from the head; and her ears were weighted down by chains and pendants, some of which also adorned her neck and hair, all jingling in time with every movement. The Italian castanets are replaced by silver bells about the ankles, which "chime light laughter around the restless feet." She raises her beautiful hand, the palms and fingers painted rosy red, and begins to propel herself in time to the music.

So far, it is just as you had expected. The dancing was the first disappointment. Here were all the best dancers in Delhi, and these were the famous dances. The girls move, attitudinize, and pose, but do not dance. It was very tiresome, the repetition of each dance by one of the four Nautch girls; and when we were informed at the end of an hour that their repertoire was exhausted, and they could only repeat the programme, we promptly declined. Far prettier were the strolling Nautch girls of the street, who danced under our window to-day, wearing beautiful rosy costumes, glittering from head to foot in tinsel, a spangled veil streaming from the head, like an Italian *regina cœli.* They look up with a smiling glance, their eyes sparkling and bright, give a gracious salaam, and become at once entirely absorbed in the dance; their slender forms bend and sway and pose, and postures follow in quick succession, but with what grace, what art, what lovely curves and infinity of bewitching attitudes! The charm deepens into surprise; astonished, you clasp your hands and watch breathlessly a childish figure take a graceful position, throw back her head, sink it slowly to the ground, pick up a silver anna with her white teeth, and rise again without apparent effort, or entanglement in her full draperies. It was a scene, the color, atmosphere, and effect, as if taken from a framed Gérome in the Luxembourg; after this, I felt that before I should again see anything so perfect, Time would indeed have a chance to throw "a dart at me."

CHAPTER XV.

JEYPORE, THE CITY OF THE RAJPUTS.

February 21.

WHERE shall I find a wishing-cap that will transport me *à volonté* to this roseate city? Fancy a seven-gated wall, topped by stone turrets, between pierced screens, enclosing a broad, airy city built of pink-and-white stucco and marble. In moments you liken it to a confectionery village,— a rosy fondu with sugar decorations; and the cinnamon-skinned natives to gingerbread men. The architecture is called Hindu Saracenic, but the style fills your mind much more with images of fairy tales. Through these broad streets, lanes, and squares nothing changes; every building is mellow, and softly outlined with open Arabesque galleries edging the flat roofs. Jeypore is like another world. I might as well write about Babylon, Sodom, or Nineveh. Driving through the town you see just what were the occupations of ancient Corinth or any other Biblical town. Here, on the street corners, squatting on the ground, are the

A GRAIN BAZAAR.

money-changers, their piles of pice and coin spread out on a mat before them. An Indian rupee is divided into sixteen annas; each anna represents four pice; every pice, three pies: and from the initial letters of the metal coinage — rupees, annas, pice — originated the expression, "Don't care a rap." In the bazaars, the lowest coins are reduced to shells, which are again subdivided into seeds, — the currency of the natives.

Farther on are the grain-dealers, sifting lovely grains through a straw pan, which fall on the bare ground; while a boy with a long bamboo pole, with a bit of muslin on the end, is frightening away hundreds of crows to prevent their stealing the scattered kernels. In the middle of the open squares pigeons are feasting in great numbers where the camels rested with their bundles of grain the night before. There are fifty times as many here as in Venice. The streets are filled with men and women, busy, and contented apparently with primitive life. It would be very natural for an ancient Hebrew to take up his abode here. If he would go to the house-top to pray, here are the flat roofs made for the purpose; if he cared for exercise, he could mount one of the dromedaries waiting about the streets, and in the pleasure of a gentle trot, camel-back, forget the "inspired monotony" of the Eastern harp. Women, in coral-tinted saris dyed a lovely shade called Sangamir, grinding flour, were a common picture. Two girls sitting on the roadside, a stone between them, their two arms clasped about a peg in the centre, are grinding a heap of grain, which rolls out higher and higher from under the stone, and mixes with the dust of the street. Their various movements are charming,—leaning forward and retreating to the even buzz of the stone as it turns on its wooden axis.

This is the most Oriental town we have seen. Men still wear their armor,—shield and swords of steel inlaid with iron and gold,—and are actually mounted on horses, their saddles striped with silver and gold, and gay fringes hanging from the reins. Elephants tread softly about the streets, wearing a double collar of tinkling bells to warn the people. In the evening their keepers bring them to drink from the fresh street fountains. At only one well is there a modern faucet for drawing water. The Mahometans, like all the natives, are utterly opposed to this innovation, and continue to draw the water by slowly letting down a rope, to which is attached a leather bucket; for time is nothing to an Eastern mind, neither is the saving of it. One evening a funny thing happened while a man was drawing up the bucket; with one twist the thirsty animal seized the faucet, turned on the water, and applying his long trunk to the fresh-running stream, contentedly drank his fill. The accents of his reproachful grunts seemed to say very plainly to his black companion, the keeper, "Conservatism is all very fine, sounds well; but if we Orientals keep our heads above water, we must make these infidel inventions serve us to do it."

As regards sentiment, the origin of the Rajputs is as delightfully unreal and brilliant as their rosy city is romantic. The traditions of Rajputana are described by Talboys Wheeler, who tells us so delightfully what I have condensed in a few words. The Rajputs, or sons of the Rajahs, whose ancestors won their spurs of victories over aboriginal, pre-Aryan races since the dawn of history, and who date back to the sun and moon, would smile at the claims of Norman blood. The Rajputs founded independent kingdoms, resembling feudal institutions, acknowledging the usual allegiance to the great Rajah, or Maharajah, whose exact connection with the *thakoors*, or nobles, was of a patriarchal nature; and to this day the lowest among the people call him "my father." The legendary war of the "Mahabharata" relates in the Sanscrit language the famous contest between the Kauravas and Pandavas, the descendants of a king of Delhi. According to tradition, the Pandavas brothers gained the victory, and the eldest gave all the Rajahs a great feast, — slaughtered a horse, and duly roasted its flesh before the fire,—a sign to all men that he had become sovereign over all the land of the Rajputs. Now, for five centuries the clans have absolutely no history that you can find out; and, therefore, like other nations in like circumstances, we are left to suppose them correspondingly happy.

But all this time *Kshatriyas* (warriors) were training for future opportunities in the use of spears and bows, the Brahmins chanted the sacred Vedas, and the condition of the poor Sudras did not differ materially from the peasant of to-day; for the great Epic has drawn tight the Eastern line of caste, which has never yet been slackened. For already the *Brahmins* (priests) appear in the highest rank, for they proceeded from the head of Brahma; then the *Kshatriyas*, or soldiers; next in importance sprang from his mighty arms the *Vaisyas*, or merchants, who represent the Creator's third choice; while the *Sudras*, or cultivators, were only given the chance to crawl out from under his feet; and the rest of mankind were left to cast their lot in one of these four divisions.

There came a time, however, when the mighty aristocracy of Rajputana endured the fall,—said to be the consequence of pride. About the tenth century of our era the old Rajput kingdom was invaded by a strong race of Tartars, against whom there was no standing. The elephants employed by the Hindus to charge the enemy, maddened by the Mahometan arrows, turned on the Rajput army, and trampled them down. After this the ancient cities on the Jumna and Ganges were deserted, and their chief founded his court at Chitor, where the old fortress still stands in the centre of this native state. Though belonging to the conquered race, the Maharanee of Chitor never consented to make a *mésalliance* with the Mogul. At this time Al-ud-Deen was Sultan of Delhi, and was bent on a conquest of Chitor, influenced by certain conventional reasons which make love and war almost identical in history. There are always the same wronged affections to be righted, and always the same melancholy maid to be rescued; and the mighty sword invariably does it,—a custom which even modern civilization has as yet tried in vain to dispel.

A strange thing is said now to have happened; but I will not ask you to accept the story, which relates that during the siege of their town for the possession of the Hindu princess, the Rajputs at Chitor resisted the Mahometans until they were starved out, and there was no alternative but to die or surrender. At last they resolved to perform a terrible rite of self-sacrifice, which was not unfrequent in ancient times, and was known as the *johur.* Huge piles of timber were raised up in a declivity, and set on fire. The women approached in a funeral procession, and threw themselves into the flames. The men arrayed themselves in saffron-colored garments, and rushed out of the fortress, sword in hand. Most of the warriors were cut to pieces; but a few escaped through the Mahometan lines, and made their way to the Ararulli Mountains. The flame and smoke of the horrible sacrifice was still rising above the hecatomb of female victims when Al-ud-Deen made his way through the heaps of slaughtered Rajputs into the old rock fortress of Chitor.

His Highness, the Maharajah of Jeypore, is said to be the thirty-ninth descendant in unbroken line from Rama, who was himself an incarnation of Vishnu, the most commendable member of the Hindu trinity; and it is certain that the dynasties of Jeypore have occupied the throne since the end of the tenth century. These pretensions to a remote antiquity are pleasantly acknowledged by day, in the homage paid to Surya-Vasni, "the Children of the Sun."

Near the Tripolia Gate is the imperial residence of Rogit Singh,—a perfect subject for the brush of Zamaçois,—the soft light falling on rosy arches and pavements and towers, the greenest of gardens making beautiful every open space, but all the time owing its greatest charm to the rich, warm

GATEWAY MAHARAJAH'S PALACE.

color. The stables are the feature of the place, and came as a refreshing relief from temples and palaces; and as we had seen but few fine horses in India, I regret not being able to see those more thoroughly. The Maharajah elephants number about one hundred. The fighting ones were kept in confinement; but others were being exercised leisurely in open spaces in the palace rear,—great, splendid creatures, with large ears, painted gold and red in diamond patterns, and many rows of tinkling bells hung around the neck. We stopped the carriage, and B. and I exclaimed, "This is the best of all, not a step farther will we go;" and the mother nodded approvingly, as usual.

In no other city in the world is the architecture so fantastic, so audaciously original. Every quarter of Jeypore has an infinite number of quaint minarets and frescoed galleries peculiar to itself. It is this freshness and originality which attracts you. There are no marvels like the Taj or the Pearl Musjid at Delhi, everything here is stucco, but has an indescribable beauty all its own. The most beautiful of the palaces, as it soars above everything else, is the Hawa-Mahal, "the Hall of the Winds." It rises like a fairy palace of fresh almond blossoms, five stories, and all tapering gracefully towards the soft blue sky, with hundreds of little balconies and overhanging windows and kiosks, every one screened with fretwork, topped with innumerable small flags. This is the royal zenana,—an unknown and mysterious palace, a seraglio, an immense monastery "whose religion is pleasure and whose god is the Maharajah." No wonder an English duchess, when visiting Jeypore, craved a sight of these pearls of the East,—the Peris, the Nourmahals, and the Cashmere beauties. A story current in Jeypore, relates that her Highness of Connaught so horrified the Maharajah by a request to see his harem that it required the utmost diplomacy on the part of England to appease his injured dignity.

Another day we spent at the Jeypore museum,—a new hall built in memory of the visit of the Prince of Wales, and filled with specimens of Indian workmanship. The gardens have cages for tigers, lions, and almost every species of Indian wild beast. The tigers are man-eaters, very beautifully striped, and quite unlike the animals one sees in menageries. We stopped to see the cheetah,—the hunting leopard,—employed by sportsmen to hunt the antelope. It was tied to a charpoy by the roadside. The leopard gracefully consented to be stroked and admired; and so easily has this habit become second nature in the East, I pulled out my purse and tossed some pice to his cheetahship on the spot, expecting to hear the animal exclaim in the usual whine, "Backsheesh, Mem Sahib, backsheesh." I solemnly declare, to my utmost dismay, the cheetah glared at me, and B. laughed heartily.

The tallest building in Jeypore is the *lat*, or tower, raised by the Rajah Istre, who gave it his name. From all points in the city it is the most striking feature of every view, towering above temples and house-tops, exciting your curiosity a dozen times a day, until you have gone, as it were, to the root of it, and have looked long and approvingly at it,—being a woman, and having heard its romantic story, which begins quite familiarly: "Once upon a time" there reigned in Jeypore a prince, who, being very young and very intelligent, held his own views about matrimony. One day he saw from his window a lovely Banniah girl, and fell desperately in love with her. This created a fine sensation in the town, and caused great alarm to the Grand Vizier, who immediately called a goodly gathering of nobles, who of course disapproved *en bloc*,—for, as usually happens in such affairs, the current of true love runs most decidedly contrary. But although the Rajah renounced the marriage, he set to work at once to outwit the Vizier; and commanded a lofty tower to be erected near her dwelling, where he spent his days watching his inaccessible sweetheart grind her corn.

February 22.

One is never tired of hearing about these Rajputs; and I listened to-day to a story from the lips of a Scotch minister of much influence here,—a man who sits on the Maharajah's left at the durbars. He said, "You know my friend who was burned yesterday? He was the second peer of the realm, descendant of a great family, a Rajput, dating far back to the very creation of the sun. A few days ago three of us were standing at his bedside,—the prime minister, Rao, first noble of Jeypore, and myself. My friend had been very ill, but from my small medical knowledge I thought him better, and so assured the young nobleman. He was a splendid fellow; and often I would walk to his house in the warm season, and find him in the evening, after a meeting of the Council of State, sitting, as is the custom, on the floor, in his native white drapery of fine linen, reading from the Bible. Often and often I have found him so reading. But now he would not listen to our assurances of recovery. He waves his hands impatiently to dismiss such a thought, and says, 'Take me, my friends, to the field of battle. I only ask to die in action like my ancestors; or move me away from a bed of sickness to die alone, bravely, and not a burden to you, my best friends.' Then I said, 'Thakoor, it is true your ancestors died in battle, but it is for you to be so brave as to suffer sickness, and show yourself to be a true and brave Rajput.' Then he quietly instructed us to have his sons take a high degree at Government College. He was very wealthy, owner of villages and great estates. We told him smilingly he would soon be well; but he had a presentiment at that moment that he should die. To-day my friend is dead.

"Some years ago he came to me, slapped me gayly on the back, and said, 'Padre Sahib, in my fields I have a garden of chillies. Now they are sown, I will watch them; and when the sun has turned the fruit to crimson, I will send the chillies to the market. And this I said when the field was sown, "All the profits I will give to Padre Sahib;" and here are one hundred and sixty rupees, eight annas, and two pice. Will you take them, Padre Sahib?' Then a thought suddenly came to me, and I said, 'Would you like me to use this money for a Bible-cart?' 'As you wish, Padre Sahib.' And with the money I had a cart made and paid a man for one year to drive it, selling the books about the streets of Jeypore,—a living monument to the man you know, who was burned yesterday in his own garden. Sometimes eighty Bibles are thus sold in one month,—and 'he was a heathen.'"

CHAPTER XVI.

AN ELEPHANT RIDE TO AMBER.

February 23.

THIS morning I was awakened very early by a voice calling through the keyhole of my bedroom door, "Six o'clock, Mem Sahib; time for chota-hazri." And soon after an Oriental brought me in a tray with tea and toast, with which begins the day for India as invariably as the sun. But we were quite disrespectful to that breakfast, scarcely glanced at it, eager not to lose a moment of the pleasure before us, — an elephant ride to Amber, the ancient but deserted capital of Jeypore.

The morning was very beautiful, — the sky clear, every green thing freshness itself. Our road was bordered by tall cactus-plants, making a wonderful hedge, all budding, ready in another week to burst out in red flowers. The drive wound through a valley, on either side were mountains gray and bleak, like the castle-crowned peaks of Lower Italy. Hundreds of peacocks were flying from branches of the mango-trees, alighting on the domes of the mosques

AN EKHA, JEYPORE.

and shrines so frequent in the East. Indeed, the most striking characteristic of every scene in Northern India is a rounded dome; it is what the wayside cross is to Italy, and the white church-spire to New England. Up in the tamarinds troops of monkeys chatter and frolic; and among the ancient carvings, green parrots, grown fearless by long security, have settled in flocks, as if by some secret instinct just where their color would harmonize and contrast with the asoka-trees, which only blossom, their poets say, when touched by the foot of a Brahmin girl; and there were plenty of partridges also, perfectly unmolested and without game laws, too. Over our heads pigeons fly in solid masses, and dip down and spread a light gray patch over the country. The whole place is buzzing, humming, and resonant with the wild life of birds and animals in this great free Zoo. Now and then a large bird stalks fearlessly along on the edge of the marshes,—a tempting mark for the sportsman. If a gun were raised, it would be instantly lowered. Why? It is a lyre-bird, which mates only once in its life; and if shot, the living bird would always be a widow. The road is lined with streams of creaking wagons, or *ekhás*, with purdahs lowered, and drawn by superb white bullocks. Sometimes, the women, hidden from sight, manage to get their little look at the outside world through a large slit, shaped like a button-hole, quite in the centre of the curtain; by inserting their small fingers, and by dint of spreading them quite wide, they can separate the opening a little more than the "law allows."

After a drive of four miles we reached the enormous black elephants provided by the Maharajah of Jeypore, who were resting and waiting for us under a banyan-tree. What sport we had in mounting! Now, ever since I arrived in India I have been pining to ride an elephant. Here, at last, is one before me,—a splendid black fellow; his ears decorated, likewise his fine head, with paint of brightest colors in queer Indian-rug designs. The next thing was to mount. The keeper touched him on his forehead with his hook; the beast obediently began to lower himself, but very deliberately, and went down on his knees, still looking like a mountain. We did not waste a moment. B. was the first to lie out luxuriously in the houdah in dreamy repose, and I was soon beside her. The mahout manages his elephant craft with a sharp, two-pointed hook, and one prick is the signal to rise.

The line of country we followed that morning was extraordinarily pretty and Eastern. The distant hills rolled gently down to the ground over which we rode. Every now and then we passed a string of camels, each one tied by the nose to the tail of the one in front. What would not one give to walk like the men and women we meet straggling towards the town! How beautifully erect they hold themselves! and the same can be said for their bearing. They are carrying bundles of grain in a linen sheet, tied once in a knot; and we notice that the grain which remained on the edge in filling the bundle has not stirred or tumbled off in the long journey. They are the vainest of races,—these women; there are touches of it among the lower orders; the mirror-rings worn on the thumbs testify to that. We saw often a group of holiday makers in a grove by the roadside,—the women in gayly-embroidered head-sheets (*phoulicaries*), sparkling with bits of mirrors inserted in the pattern, and the children tumbling around on the grass, wearing brightest tinsel caps and jackets. All these people have come here to do "poojah" to the idol. Close beside is the shrine, all garlanded with green creepers and flowering vines, where sagacious Ganesh, "the elephant god," is looking wise and very shiny in a fresh coat of brilliant red paint, bestowed on him by a devout Hindu worshipper.

After a few more miles of hills, we slowly approach beautiful Amber,—Amber, with its undulating site, the mellow tones of its ancient castle reflected in a hazy lake, and its turrets vaguely outlined against the mountain background.

The elephant winds up the narrow roadway, almost brushing us off at the narrow portals; and a bell rings to announce that we have reached the very top. An echo repeats the sound, and the frightened peacocks fly buzzing through the air, like a long comet, — a sweep of green and blue. Suddenly we realize that there is not one human being for miles who can speak English or anything else except Urdu. Shanker had remained in charge of the carriage. Here we were in Central India, with two Eastern servants and a keeper of elephants, on the landing of the stairway to a deserted palace, with only the still and silent creatures who lived there moving about as in a dream. And the faint, far-away bell rang once, as if to summon up the dead spirits of warrior Rajputs who lived here ages ago. "Summon" is the word which seems most in touch with the enchanted palace; and we had a strong conviction that they would be on hand if needed. The palace surrounds a large square, where hundreds of buffaloes are sacrificed every year to Kali. A servant comes up, and motions us to follow him. Straightway we mount a long stairway, and at the end are signalled to remove our shoes; "for the place on which we stand is holy ground." From a dark recess glares a dark-blue image, in full skirts of gold cloth. It is Devi, the Destroyer. The priest was, as usual, idling about; two women were piously prostrated in adoration. The shrine was lined with flowers, and sputtering candle-ends burnt low in brass saucers,—a bit of Italy in Indian masquerade. An icy marble floor was chilling us through and through. We stopped only long enough to toss a rupee to each attendant priest, and were soon walking through endless marble rooms. The names have slipped my memory. In time the guide marshalled us to a lovely apartment, where a shimmer of light flooded the room,—a mirror-room; exquisitely carved Saracenic arches were studded with gold-edged bits of looking-glass. The room was known as the "Shish Mahal."

From an upper gallery you look down on the most wonderful view in all the world. Just below is an emerald lake, dotted with islands, where wild peacocks with sunlit plumage dart from the thick shrubbery. The near hills seem to fold about the little brown-and-gray town of Amber, as if to protect her precious old ruins. The green of spring and summer is only half suggested now, but the warm soil-tints make up for the fresh green of young grass. All sizes of monkeys run wild over temples and niches, and jump from tree to tree in perfect liberty to follow their own will and wish. The distant hills are enchantingly beautiful; every pinnacle crested with castles, violet and brownish in the soft atmosphere of an Indian morning. We can trace the road we have just passed over, and can see more elephants curving down the hill-sides. In another moment we are taking one lingering farewell look at Amber, and pass out and beyond the palace gateway. Suddenly, close by my side, a harsh voice breaks the stillness: "Good critics refuse to acknowledge the charm of Amber. Its palace is a mere mass of stucco,—a florid horror to be escaped from as quickly as possible." It was one of the tourists, whose elephant we had seen approaching, reading from a guide-book.

BOMBAY, February 28.

At the Esplanade Hotel once more. We travelled from Jeypore direct, stopped at Ahmedabad for dinner, and the second morning pulled up into Church-gate Station, Bombay. Mr. K. found us out, and asked us to dine at the Yacht Club; and we sailed with him one afternoon to Elephanta Island.

We left the Apollo Bunder about three in the afternoon; and at the end of an hour and a half arrived at a low woody island nearly opposite to Bombay. The landing-place is so difficult of approach, on account of the pointed rocks near the shore and the shallowness of the water, that we were told the natives formerly waded out to the boat, and took the passengers ashore on their backs. A souvenir of one of the lordly visits to the East, of its far-away English masters, is a path of smooth-hewn rocks built out in the water, forming a sort of pier, through which the water rushes, and over which you are obliged to jump from one wet and slippery stone to another to reach the island. I had formed a picture in my mind as to what Elephanta would be like, and found it almost a fac-simile. The side of a small mountain has been excavated to the depth of several hundred feet, leaving natural pillars of the solid rock, which form the aisles of the stony basilica. The sides are sculptured in a series of events, describing the life of Siva. These have been so injured by time, tide, and the Portuguese, who drew their cannon up to the entrance and fired destroying blasts, that they are no longer beautiful or interesting, except to an archæologist or naturalist; for one sees here specimens of every known snake crawling about the pools or in the dark recesses of the temple.

From Elephanta we return in the steam-launch to Bombay; and we convince ourselves with difficulty that this brings our days in India to a close "as a tale that is told." And when I look back, I would dwell on them, encore every one, and live over again each hour; and were the offer made me, would retrace the journey step by step before it becomes a dream and the memory of it a wish. A journey comes to an end; every one's passage is taken homeward sooner or later, by steamer or by Charon's Ferry; but the events and happenings have become a part of our lives, have influenced them forever. Two long lines of smoke blow over the harbor from the steamship "Ganges," bound for Egypt. Yes, it is a fact that this is our last night in Bombay, and the last page of my journal. How hurried and imperfect are these impressions! — the faintest hint of real feeling. Shall I ever be able to trace the subtle poetry and magic of India from a bit of writing, a scrap of an hour here, or a day there, when all is left unsaid that could make it a reality? And, above all, shall anything in these pages induce you to go to the East? If not, what have you gained from "A Girl's Winter in India"?

THE END.